BIBLIA CABALISTICA

or

The Cabalistic Bible

SHOWING HOW THE VARIOUS NUMERICAL CABALAS HAVE BEEN
CURIOUSLY APPLIED TO THE HOLY SCRIPTURES, WITH NUMEROUS TEXTUAL
EXAMPLES RANGING FROM GENESIS TO THE APOCALYPSE, AND COLLECTED
FROM BOOKS OF THE GREATEST RARITY, FOR THE MOST PART NOT IN THE
BRITISH MUSEUM OR ANY PUBLIC LIBRARY IN GREAT BRITAIN

WITH INTRODUCTION, APPENDIX OF CURIOS AND BIBLIOGRAPHY

Rev. Walter Begley

ISBN 1-56459-017-8

Kessinger Publishing's Rare Reprints
Thousands of Scarce and Hard-to-Find Books!

- - -
- - -
- - -
- - -
- - -
- - -
- - -
- - -
- - -
- - -
- - -
- - -
- - -
- - -
- - -
- - -
- - -
- - -
- - -
- - -

We kindly invite you to view our extensive catalog list at:
http://www.kessinger.net

PREFACE

THERE is little need for an extended preface to this book, for the title-page shows very plainly its purport and the nature of the contents. I would simply say here, that the following pages are chiefly intended for lovers and collectors of literary curiosities, a class of readers who are, I believe, on the increase nowadays. People with such tastes do not so much care for the books "which," they are told, "no gentleman's library should be without," as for books that are curious, paradoxical, out of the common run, and not before met with in the course of their reading. This book should therefore well meet their requirements. And I can only hope that it will also succeed in attracting the attention and satisfying the curiosity of a few, at least, of that somewhat eccentric band of bibliophiles whose ranks I joined some years ago, and have never regretted my enlistment.

CONTENTS

INTRODUCTION

INTRODUCTION

I AM rather afraid that the title will scarcely give a correct idea of the contents of this book, for there is an old cabala and a new cabala, and these two are very different. The first is mainly Hebrew, and occasionally Greek ; the second is almost entirely Latin, and of much later invention, not being heard of till about A.D. 1530. The old cabala *per gematriam*, as it was technically spoken of, is well known to Biblical scholars everywhere. The new cabala is scarcely mentioned in any books of reference, and the works containing specimens of it are rare in the highest degree ; this latter fact accounting for the general want of knowledge on the subject. What I mean by saying that the title may convey a wrong idea is that ninety-nine persons out of a hundred would think of the old Hebrew and Greek cabala and the Jewish fancies therein displayed, whereas our *Biblia Cabalistica* has mainly to do with the record of Christian fancy on Christian themes ; while here the Latin tongue is the one chiefly used. It matches my *Biblia Anagrammatica*, and runs on exactly parallel lines with it, being a collection of Bible texts treated in this case *cabalistically*, as they are in that case *anagrammatically*, and therefore I could hardly choose any other title.

However, I have not failed to notice in an appendix at the end of this book some of the strongest and most interesting examples of the older cabala, so I hope that readers who only expected this will not be altogether disappointed.

Moreover, some general remarks on this more ancient part of the subject are needed now, to begin with, as an introduction to the whole.

3

MYSTICAL AND CABALISTIC NUMBERS IN THE ANCIENT SCRIPTURES OF THE OLD AND NEW TESTAMENT.

This curious branch of theological science has been investigated and discussed by many writers, ancient and modern, and quite recently two writers, Dr. Bullinger and Mr. J. H. Weldon, have gone deeply into the matter and added many curious coincidences not before noticed.

The instances given by them are by no means of equal value, and some are not very convincing. But their cabalistic deductions from some of the numbers of the Bible, notably 8, 13, and 153, are so remarkable and novel that I have included the best of them in my survey of the cabalistic numbers in the appendix. To readers not conversant with *gematria* they will be a surprise, and, taken in connection with other instances adduced, will, I think, be sufficient to show that there may very possibly be something more than mere *random* fancy in the way many special numbers and names of Holy Writ are used by the original writers. Personally, I claim no more from my inferences than this, although many professed students go much farther.

Anyhow, the following statement is unobjectionable : " The symbolical meaning of numbers in Holy Scripture deserves more study and attention than it has received in recent times." This is a remark of Dr. Christopher Wordsworth, a learned and judicious scholar, who was the very reverse in every way of an extreme man. It was made some years ago, and since then the science of theology has made such rapid progress, in this as well as in other directions, that nowadays one can venture boldly to say that even the cabala of the Bible deserves more study than it has received. It has been dismissed almost universally as the vainest and most unproductive of literary follies. All educated men of evenly balanced minds were virtually in agreement in their view that there was not and could not be any magic power or significance in *gematria* or the counting of a name or text, and all people who took interest in such puerile fancies were either stupidly superstitious or grossly ignorant in their conceptions of what true knowledge was.

As so often happens in the matter of literary judgments, and other judgments as well, these cultivated and judicious men were both right and wrong. They were right according to the lights and knowledge of their age, and their judgment was sane according to the evidence before them. But there was a great deal of evidence not before them, which has since come to light and made their opinion, which was once relatively right, become now relatively wrong.

In days gone by, no one thought of looking upon a Primitive Christian in the light of an initiate with mysterious knowledge carefully conveyed and concealed. To all Churchmen, High or Low, Primitive Christians became " wise unto salvation " by about the same or somewhat similar means as Primitive Methodists become converted men nowadays. This was the current idea—true enough in a certain sense, of course, but withal very misleading, for how much of importance was overlooked or unknown !

The various complicated ways in which the earliest Christianity was brought into connection with the Greek, Mithraic, and other mysteries, is almost a study of the last half-century, and has a by no means unimportant connection with mystic names and numbers. And the same may be said of the Essenes, the Neo-Pythagoreans, and all the many embryonic forms of Gnosticism, which were, like microbes, " in the air," naturally infecting more or less every religious growth within their sphere of influence, according as the *nidus* was suitable or not. The disputants of past generations were unaware of most of these things.

And yet the Primitive Christian was an initiate plainly enough, and had a *disciplina arcani* even as other initiates. But the Christian mysteries had this advantage over other mysteries : there was with them the open door ; for behold, the " door was opened in heaven " and on earth. That is to say, Christianity was an initiation of a more universal character than was allowed in the Eleusinian mysteries or any of the various other mystic rites which multiplied to an unusual extent just before and after the Christian era. In Christ Jesus there was no bar of birth, nationality, or even of moral conduct. " Whosoever will, let him come " ; " Where there is neither Greek nor Jew, circumcision nor uncircumcision, Barbarian, Scythian, bond nor free." Sinners, slaves, and outcasts were invited to come freely. Women, too, debarred from the great mysteries of Paganism, were accepted here on equal terms. In Christ Jesus there was neither male nor female.

I believe that this acceptance of the woman—virgin, wife, and widow—on almost equal terms to the rites and ceremonies and religious privileges of the new religion, had more to do with the rapid progress and final triumph of early Christianity than is generally supposed. The great reason is not sufficiently dwelt upon by the critics and historians of the Rise and Progress of our Faith. Women comprise half, or more than half, of the human race, and their susceptibilities to a religion of faith and hope are much stronger and more persistent than those of the sterner sex. Even allowing that with women these feelings are less sceptical and critical than with men, we must not forget that religions rise and advance not by the dry critical faculty so much as by the imaginative enthusiasm of the *anima naturaliter pia*. Besides, would not a religion of love and peace appeal more to the impulsive woman than to the fierce warrior or the subtle logician?

Many of the early Christians had, no doubt, been initiates, and when converted to the new method of salvation—that *Soteria* so many were seeking in those days of religious revival—they would readily understand the mystic or cryptic allusions in the writings of the New Testament, especially when written by converted initiates, as the writers of the Epistle to the Colossians and the Apocalypse most probably were.

The mystic numbers of Daniel and the Apocalypse would be no new ground to initiates and deep religious inquirers. The philosophy of the ancients was greatly geometrical. It is a reported dictum of Plato that God Himself γεωμετρεῖ, and it was the mark of the wise to understand hierophantic and other mysteries, and to deliver them in turn (Παράδοσις). It was esoteric knowledge not meant for those that were without, and therefore there was a certain concealment to preserve such matters from profane eyes; but it was the duty and privilege of the "wise" within the fold, of those who had "understanding," to "count the number" and possess the secret. Besides the cryptic signs known by tradition to the initiates, there was cryptic astrology as well. Many of the mystic numbers in the Bible are connected with astronomy, the motions of the heavenly bodies, the yearly motion of the sun (as it was then thought) through the constellations, etc.

The signs in the Apocalypse are manifestly taken from the heavenly bodies, and indeed we learn from the first chapter of Genesis that one of the purposes for which these heavenly luminaries were created was to be for "signs," and this purpose was put first in the sacred text. Therefore we should not be too ready to say, as many do, that these remarkable cabalistic coincidences were not originally intended by the writers, but have been extracted from the text by the ingenious fancy and device of men who found what they looked for.

We may admit that ingenious manipulation of words and numbers has sometimes—nay, often—brought out what was never intended, but there is an honest residuum, too clear, too precise, and too startling to be anything but positively indicative of the cryptic cabalism of the Biblical writers. Many of the composers of the sacred books of the Bible, the compilers, too, of the Gospels, and especially the Revelators. such as Daniel and John, would feel bound by the nature of their themes to be cryptic and cabalistic and esoteric. To take one simple instance : " And the *third* day there was a *marriage* in *Cana* of *Galilee* ; and the *mother* of Jesus was there." My strong opinion is that this is throughout a cryptic statement of an esoteric character, that there is much more in it than appears to the ordinary reader, and that by the words I have italicised, and farther on in the narrative as well, the writer intended to convey to the " wise " some theological or spiritual truth which was widely different from the account of a provincial wedding feast. And I think the same remark will hold good with regard to the herd of swine that ran violently down a steep place into the sea (the deep, the abyss ?) and were choked.

It is just because we do not know what the cryptic teaching of such narratives is, that they seem so strange to us in the Bible, and make the faith of many grow cold.

It was ignorance of these things that nearly broke off the engage-. ment between the famous Dr. Bentley, Master of Trinity, and his affianced lady, Miss Joanna Bernard, whom he first met at Bishop Stillingfleet's house, from which latter fact we might infer that she was severely orthodox.

It seems she was much alarmed one day by some expressions her learned lover used with regard to the measurements of the golden image which Nebuchadnezzar the king had set up. They seemed to her to cast a doubt on the authority of the Book of Daniel. Whiston has told

us what Bentley's alarming assertion was. The image is described as
sixty cubits high, and six cubits broad. "Now," said Bentley, "this is
out of all proportion ; it ought to have been ten cubits broad at least."
This, we are told, "made the good lady weep." It has been supposed
that this lovers' difference was amicably arranged on the basis suggested
by Whiston—that the sixty cubits included the pedestal. Anyhow, they
lived a happy wedded life together for forty years, and considering the
Master of Trinity's determined temper and almost lifelong worries, we
may well agree with Professor Jebb (Bentley, p. 98) when he says,
"Perhaps, if all were known, few women ever went through more in
trying, like Mrs. Thrale, to be civil for two."

But what a regrettable incident if forty happy years of married life
had really thus been sacrificed, through both parties being ignorant of
the mystical and cabalistic meaning of the number 6 !

It was the ordinary method in all mysteries for the hierophants or
mystagogues to convey hidden truths by means of a more or less obvious
fiction. They would thus use a myth, or parable, or significant number,
to conceal the inner meaning, and, as an anonymous writer has said very
recently, " It has come to pass that the crude and childish lie on the
surface is ignorantly believed for the whole truth, instead of being
recognised as the mere clue to its inner meaning. All theology is
composed in this way, and her twofold utterances must be read with
a double mind. Thus, when we read in the Scriptures of the Church,
or in the saintly legends, a fiction showing more than ordinary
exuberance of fancy, we may be sure that our attention is being specially
arrested. When miraculous events are related of the gods, or when they
are depicted in marvellous shapes, the author gives us to understand that
something uncommon is being conveyed. When singular and unearthly
beasts are described such as Behemoth and Leviathan, the unicorn or the
phœnix, it is intended that we should search deeply into their meaning :
for such are some of the artifices by which the ancients at once concealed
and explained their hidden mysteries." *

As far as the Old Testament is concerned, it has been supposed
that some astronomical science of the Hebrews is mystically concealed

* *The Canon* (Lond. 1897), p. 10.

under the figures of Noah's Ark, the Tabernacle, the Temple of
Solomon, and the Holy Oblation of Ezekiel. In the New Testament it
is thought that the Christians added to these the mystical city of the
New Jerusalem described in the last two chapters of the Revelation.

It seems clear that Daniel's numbers are in some way astronomical,
and the same holds with many of the numbers of the Apocalypse dealing
with the consummation of the age, while *gematria* was evidently a part
of the esoteric teaching in the early New Testament days, as appears
from the number of the Beast, and from what we read in the Epistle
of Barnabas (chap. ix.) concerning the number of Abraham's servants,
which was 318 : " For scripture says that Abraham circumcised 318
men of his house. But what was the mystery that was made known
unto him ? Mark first the 18, and next the 300. For the numerical
letters of 10 and 18 are IH. And these denote ʹIH(ΣΟΤΣ). And
because the Cross was that by which we were to find grace, therefore he
adds 300 ; the note of which is T (the figure of his cross). Wherefore
by two letters he signified Jesus, and by the third his cross. He knows
this who has put the engrafted gift of his doctrine within us. No one
has learned a more genuine word from me than this, but I know that ye
are worthy of it."

This is ingenious, but the later rabbis have, in a midrash, I think
surpassed it. For they, finding that the name of Eliezer, Abraham's
steward, was by *gematria* 318, inferred from this that Eliezer himself
stood for the 318 armed men of Abraham's household, and that
Abraham got the victory mentioned in the Bible with Eliezer alone, who
was equal to all of them, and that he left the rest of them at home.

The early Christian poet Prudentius refers to this number of
Abraham's servants in his *Psychomachia,* and adds that we, too, may be
rich in servants, and successful in our conflicts if we only comprehend
the *mystica figura* of the number 318.

The passage has been rather a *crux* with commentators, who in
their expositions have found, as did Mr. Gladstone so often, three
courses open to them :—

1. With Rupertus, Pererius, and Antonius Nebrissensis, they might
conclude that the Council of Nicæa and its 318 bishops there assembled
was the reference intended, and that the Nicene Creed was the *mystica*

figura which should so greatly avail us ; being that whereby the great opponent Arius was routed by the 318 bishops, and whereby we should prevail also if we held it fast to the end.

2. The explanation of Barnabas as recorded above.

3. The explanation that VnICa CrVCIs fIgVra was the mystic figure meant by Prudentius, which, according to the value of its Latin numerals was exactly 318—viz., three C's, three V's, and three I's.

I think No. 2 seems the most likely. The date of Prudentius is much too early for any chronogrammatic device such as No. 3, which is therefore out of court. As for the apocalyptical number 666, the amount of time and discussion that has been wasted on it is amazing.

David Thom, a Liverpool minister, composed a large octavo of more than four hundred pages on this number, and discusses many of the solutions very learnedly. Strange to say, he dismissed the most likely number of the numerous list without a remark. We shall see in the appendix how ingeniously our concealed Lutheran cabalist stamped it indelibly on one of the Popes—Leo X. The Popes have always had this bestial mark given them by Protestants, if it could possibly be fixed upon them in one way or another.

But now, surely, we know how wrong and foolish all this defaming and branding of ecclesiastical dignities is. What *had* the Apocalypse to do with the Popes ? The idea seems absurd. The Apocalypse spoke to the initiates who had " understanding." Its concern was mainly with current political events and the wondrous things soon to happen on the earth. Consequently we must not look for the solution of 666 in an ecclesiastical direction. The Popes and the Apocalypse are very far apart. Cæsar and his " Babylon," and the privileges of Roman citizenship (possibly the mark of the Beast in the hand), were the burning questions of that book and age.

There seems a great probability that Christianity was a socialistic movement as well as a religious and moral one, and herein is the explanation of the persecution of the Christians by the Cæsars, good and bad alike, Marcus Aurelius as well as Nero. The wily politicians in high places saw the democratic and socialistic danger ; and the peace-loving, brotherly community of watchful, expectant Christians saw their real and greatest enemy.

It was Rome, the second Babylon, the mother of wealth, idolatry, tyranny, and all the abominations of the earth. If the peaceable kingdom of Christ was to be set up, then the cry must first resound through the earth, " Babylon is fallen." The Sibylline books, both Jewish and Christian, point in this direction. Doubtless there were many communistic socialists and initiates among the readers of the Seer of Patmos. To them Christ was Lord, not Cæsar, and that was the ultimate test that brought so many of them to the lions and the flames. Such as they would not be very long in guessing or counting out by *gematria* that Beast which has puzzled so many generations since.

But my *Biblia Cabalistica* only touches upon the mystic numbers of the Bible incidentally. Its primary object, as already hinted, is to present to the curious reader a collection of texts from the Bible and Apocrypha, which have been treated cabalistically by ingenious authors, and which are for the most part unknown even to bookworms of considerable research. It runs strictly parallel in its method to my *Biblia Anagrammatica*, and both deal only with Bible texts throughout, the one great exception being the early Lutheran exposition of 2300, 1290, 1335, and 666, which are numbers rather than texts, and this has been added on account of its rarity and singular ingenuity, and thrown into an appendix with some other singularities connected with the numerical cabala of the Bible.

Now, when did this science or pseudo-science first make its appearance? How old is this *gematria*, this exposition of words by their numerical value, in which the Talmudic Jews, and other people before them and after them, so much delighted? I do not suppose any precise date can be given at this distance of time, and when the records of Eastern nations which might throw light on the subject are lost, or rather not yet available. For who, after our Babylonian and Egyptian finds, can dare to say we may not yet find further accounts of the rise and influence of this branch of esoteric philosophy?

However, in any case, I believe the cabala was used much earlier than most people think. We must go behind the Jews farther back into the ages to people more civilised than they were, if we wish to meet with the *prima stamina* of these curious devices. What the Eastern nations understood by the term " wisdom " dealt largely with numbers

Without going too far back into the dim past as the time when " Moses was learned in all the wisdom of the Egyptians," we may safely say that the Jews, during their captivity in Babylon, would learn the "wisdom" of the Chaldeans, and this was most distinctly numerical and astrological, connected with recurring cycles of stellar motion and times and seasons marked out by the stars and the sun's passage through them. And later on, when through the liberal treatment of the Greek Ptolemies they lived in free intercourse with the philosophers of all schools at Alexandria, the Pythagorean doctrine that *number* is the active principle and root of the visible world would doubtless be brought to their notice. Indeed, as a matter of fact, we find that very idea was current among them in some of those Biblical writings we call the Apocrypha, which really hailed not from Jerusalem, but from the Alexandrian Judaic school. A good instance is Wisdom xi. 20, where we read : "But Thou hast ordered all things in measure, and number, and weight."

The numerical cabala of the old kind was at its greatest height of favour and influence during the period beginning a century before the introduction of Christianity and ending three centuries after that event— *i.e.*, B.C. 100—A.D. 300, which period would include the later Persian, Chaldean, and Alexandrian precursors of the Gnostics, and the Gnostics themselves, who were, some of them, great cabalists, and more addicted to the art than the contemporary Jew or the Christian mystic who remained orthodox.

However, the authorities, whether Imperial or Pontifical, never looked upon this curious art with favourable eyes. To the Emperors it seemed allied to the art of the " mathematici," a class of men they hated and feared, although they consulted them. To the ecclesiastical authorities it savoured of heresy, Gnosticism, and Judaism. So it gradually fell out of favour, but it remained with the Talmudic Jew who sought after " wisdom," and it burst forth with a new light when the Zohar was found, or rather concocted, in the thirteenth century.

The mediæval Jews, too, we are told on good authority, continued to practise with great glee these old devices of their forefathers. " Another class of Jewish (mediæval) pastimes was of a more intellectual nature. Arithmetical tricks known as *gematria* were old favourites ; perhaps instances of them are not unknown in the Old Testament (cf. Stade's *Zeitschrift*, 1896, p. 122). At all events, they were very much fancied in the Middle Ages, and formed the recreation of great rabbinical scholars. The Talmud, for instance, humorously says that a good Jew must drink wine at Purim until he can no longer distinguish between 'Blessed be Mordecai' and 'Cursed be Haman.' The point of the remark was derived from the numerical identity of the Hebrew words forming the two phrases (each = 502)." *

And later on, at the beginning of the eighteenth century, I have found an instance of a Jew using the Biblical cabala in honour of a Christian prince. As this broad-minded Jew made use of the first three verses of Psalm xxi., the attempt appears in its place in the present book, and the pamphlet figures in the bibliography (*s.v.* 1701, Simon Wolff Brandes). But in these later times of the sixteenth and seventeenth centuries, it was the converted Christian ex-rabbis who made the greatest public use of the cabala, in every case with a view to convert their brethren. We are told of a cabalist (presumably a Christian) who obtained the name of Jesus (Jod, Schin, Vau) out of the dimensions of the Ark, and again out of Solomon's Temple. And the Jewish rabbi, Theodorus Genuensis, afterwards called Ludovicus Carret (he became a physician), was converted to Christianity by the wonderful cabalistic mysteries he had noticed could be drawn from the triliteral name JSV (in Hebrew). He always declared that the three-headed letter (Schin) in the middle referred to the mystery of the Trinity. W. Schickard, in his work, *Bechinath Happeruschin*, Tübingen, 1624, pp. 65-102, is my authority, and refers to a work by Rabbi Theodorus, entitled *De Visionibus Dei*. This I have not met with, but there is a book by J. Faulhaber, which I have seen, entitled *Vernunfftigen Creaturen Weissagungen*, Augsburg, 1632, where the measurements of a wonderful stag are taken, with the result that the famous prophetical numbers 666, 1260, 1335, and 2300 all come out from the horns, hoofs, and back of the portentous animal. And again, he takes a wonderful fish found on the coast of Denmark with strange characters on it, and from a cunning manipulation of these he brings out once more the Apocalyptic numbers. These marvels have always been received with marked

---

* Israel Abrahams, *Jewish Life in the Middle Ages* (London, 1896–8), p. 381.

attention by the uneducated vulgar, which I suppose accounts for their recurrence. We must remember, too, that neither the Jews nor Greeks in ancient times used special and distinct numerals as we do ; for with them the letters of the alphabet were their numerals, and therefore the number of a word was much more open to observation and calculation than with us.

The great liking that many of the Talmudic rabbis had for clinching their arguments by means of the numerical cabala is well known to Oriental students. For instance :—

(1) Rav Yehudah, the brother of Rav Salla the Holy, said : "Satan has no permission to accuse any one on the Day of Atonement. How do we know this ?" Ramma bar Chamma replied : "Satan by gematria equals 364, therefore on that number of days only has he permission to accuse ; but on the Day of Atonement (*i.e.*, the 365th day) he cannot accuse." (*Yoma*, fol. 20.)

(2) There are 903 sorts of death in the world, for the expression occurs (Psalm lxviii. 20), "Issues of death." The numerical value of "issues" is 903. The hardest of all deaths is by quinsy, and the easiest is by the Divine kiss—of which Moses, Aaron, and Miriam died. (*Berachoth*, fol. 8.)

(3) It was said by one of old time, "Blessed is he who submits to a reproach and is silent, for *a hundred* evils depart from him." Now, *strife* in Hebrew letters equals 100, which explains the particular form of the aphorism.*

This knowledge of the cabala has always been in high estimation with the bookish Jew, almost until the last century or two, and I have no doubt there are learned cabalists among the conservative Talmudists of Poland and Galicia even now. .

The cabala had two distinct branches—the practical and the theoretical. The former dealt with magic, with invocation of spirits, bad and good, by names and charms, and such-like folly of the superstitious imagination. It was naturally most in favour with the lower-class Jew and the uneducated vulgar, and this part of the cabala does not enter into our subject. The latter, or theoretical cabala, was the study of

* The above and many others can be found in Hershon's *Talmudic Miscellany*. (London, 1880, 8vo.)

rabbis and literati, and both branches attracted some notice and much odium during the period of the Early Renaissance, when alien and heretical literature were, for the first time, beginning to be freely examined by daring spirits, in spite of the ban of the ecclesiastical power.

That Admirable Crichton of his age, the famous Johannes Picus, Comes de Mirandola, went into these matters at considerable length in some of his treatises, and incurred, in consequence, much abuse from his adversaries in monkish and obscurantist coteries. They displayed their profound ignorance sometimes in a rather amusing manner; a conversation between two of these dunderheads is thus reported by our learned Count: "What is this cabala that they talk about, nowadays?" says one to his fellow. "Oh, don't you know?" says the other. "This cabala is a certain diabolically perfidious man, and that is his name; he has written many things against Christ, and so his followers are called *Cabalistæ*."*

Another authority,† some years later, gives us another answer to this self-same question, "What is this cabala?" And here we are told that "She is an old witch thoroughly practised in poisonings and enchantments." In this case it was clearly the practical cabala that the respondent was thinking of.

But all this would be vile and ignorant to the good Talmudic Jew. *His* account was a very different one. His precious cabala was part of the oral law of God given to Moses on Mount Sinai, during the night when there was no light and no stars ‡ (on account of the cloud, I suppose), and therefore nothing much to be done otherwise.

As for the origin of the modern Latin cabala, we are able to fix it much more definitely. It appears to have come into use first in Germany about the time of the Reformation (1530-50), and afterwards it took a start in Italy, chiefly in the neighbourhood of Piacenza, in the year

---

* Cum quidam interrogaretur: Quid Cabala esset? respondit: fuisse perfidum quendam hominum et diabolicum qui dicebatur CABALA, et hunc multa contra Christum scripsisse unde sequaces ejus dictos esse Cabalistas.—Picus in *Apolog.*, 116.

† Thom. Garzoni, *Il Teatro* (1549-89).

‡ In monte Sinai noctu, cum lux deficeret ob candelarum absentiam. Cf. Z. Celspirius, *de Anagr.*, Libri duo (Ratisb. 1713), p. 46.

1621. These two origins were quite independent of each other, and, indeed, the systems of counting were not the same.

In Germany they began with triangular numbers—that is, the letters were numbered according to arithmetical progression, 1, 3, 6, 10, 15, etc., which when represented by dots are all triangles increasing regularly in size, *e.g.*—

etc.

How it came about that this particular kind of *gematria* was chosen is rather singular. It happened thus : Our first worthy cabalist, who is responsible for the remarkable treatment of the Apocalyptic numbers of Daniel and St. John at the end of the present book, was an ardent Lutheran, and was possessed by the fixed idea that the Beast with the seven heads was one of the Popes, and, for preference, Leo X. Whoever it might be, this much was clear—his number must be 666. So he began to reckon by the simplest cabala, $a = 1$, $b = 2$, $c = 3$, etc., but could get nothing appropriate. He therefore increased his alphabet value by making each letter equal to the sum of all its preceding letters, and found, to his surprise and delight, that many remarkable results came out at once.

"I still remember well," he says in his cabalistical book, "how horribly this final anathema of the Pope's Bulls sounded in my ears : *qui contrafecerit, indignationem Dei omnipotentis, etc., noverit se incursurum* (Whoever shall act contrary to the tenor of this Bull shall know the wrath falling upon him). What blasphemy, thought I, that a dying miserable man (*ellender*) should dare to assert that *his* wrath was the wrath of Almighty God. Here, said I, is one of the heads of the Beast surely. And I wrote down $\overline{\text{Leo Decimus}}^{721}$ and $\overline{\text{Indignatio Dei}}^{721}$ by my cabala, and they agree and are wonderfully equal, and so I have proceeded in all my reckonings."

The *cabala trigonalis* thus singularly brought into vogue in Germany held its ground there almost to the exclusion of the simpler cabala for some time, and several at Breslau and elsewhere afterwards followed in his steps, but very far indeed from his height of excellence. The early arithmeticians, especially Boethius, had a great deal more to say about triangular and polygonal numbers than we have, and it was probably from these sources that our cabalist obtained his singular notation.

In Italy we hear nothing of any Latin cabala till nearly a century later, and then, in 1621, a circle of literary ecclesiastics started the fashion on the occasion of the left arm of Blessed Conrad, a famous hermit in his time, being brought from Netina to Piacenza.

A full account is given in the book *Anathemata B. Conrado* (Placentia, 1621), and we are even told of the first Latin cabala that was made—viz.,

$$\overset{3}{C} \overset{13}{O} \overset{12}{N} \overset{16}{R} \overset{1}{A} \overset{4}{D} \overset{19}{V} \overset{17}{S} = \overset{9}{I} \; \overset{4}{D} \overset{5}{E} \overset{3}{C} \overset{19}{V} \overset{17}{S} \; \overset{3}{C} \overset{1}{A} \overset{5}{E} \overset{10}{L} \overset{9}{I}$$

The dedication of the book is signed by Hieronymus Spadius, probably a relative of Johannes Baptista Spadius, who was a famous writer of anagrams and centones, and an early Latin cabalist as well, as may be seen by some of his Biblical attempts recorded later on in this book.

The Italian cabalists always preferred either the simple cabala :—

1	2	3	4	5	6	7	8	9	10	11	12	13	14	15	16	17	18	19	20	21	22
A	B	C	D	E	F	G	H	I	L	M	N	O	P	Q	R	S	T	U	X	Y	Z

or what is called the ordinary cabala :—

1	2	3	4	5	6	7	8	9	10	20	30	40	50	60	70	80	90	100	200	300	400	500
A	B	C	D	E	F	G	H	I	K	L	M	N	O	P	Q	R	S	T	U	X	Y	Z

I find no instance of their use of the triangular or polygonal numbers ; that was left to the Germans, and was called by them *cabala paragrammatica*.

Concerning this branch of the subject, Johann Henning wrote an interesting work in 1683, entitled *Cabbalologia*, and gives several examples composed by himself and others in triangular, square, pentagonal, heptagonal, octagonal, enneagonal, and decagonal numbers. There are no examples founded on Biblical texts, and therefore no extracts appear in the body of the present collection. But as examples of this most difficult kind of cabala, I will give one example from the square numbers and one from the pentagonal.

2

1. An epitaph for :—

Petrus Vehr, Berolinensis Marchicus.   5531

PER CAB. □

Gaude ! sic tandem itur per labores ad honores.   5531*

The cabala used being :—

$$\overset{1}{A} \quad \overset{4}{B} \quad \overset{9}{C} \quad \overset{16}{D} \quad \text{all squares up to} \quad \overset{484}{X} \quad \overset{529}{Y} \quad \overset{576}{Z}$$

2. Written when a friend of Johann Henning lost his son, *Frederick Christian* :—

Fridrich Christianus.   4358

PER CAB. ⬠

Pace Dei vere tutus.   4358

$$\overset{1}{A} \quad \overset{5}{B} \quad \overset{12}{C} \quad \overset{22}{D} \quad \text{all pentagonal to} \quad \overset{715}{X} \quad \overset{782}{Y} \quad \overset{852}{Z}$$

Besides Henning, there was no German paragrammatist till about thirty years later, when Johann Friederich Riederer, of Augsburg, published a rough list of what he had done in this branch. His *paragrammata cabalistica* were all in triangular numbers, and in the vernacular mainly. They were fashionable compositions connected with the German courts and upper classes, and originally appeared in such publications as court gazettes and similar journals. His list gave the subjects of 1050 specimens of his art and the Bible texts he chose to illustrate cabalistically, but the complete cabalas are not given. As a rule,

---

* I would call attention to the excellence of this and the following example concerning the son who was *in pace*. Two of the best and most widely-known literal anagrams are :—

    Florence Nightingale = Flit on, cheering angel.
    Horatio Nelson   = Honor est a Nilo.

But the difficulty of composing a literal anagram is very much less than is the case with cabala, especially with quadrangular and pentagonal ones. Since the result above is equally as neat and appropriate as the best anagrams can give, we may esteem the above cabala to be very remarkable ones.

I should say they were not published, but sent privately to friends and patrons interested. However, some few found their way into the gazettes as above mentioned, and I have collected these from several out-of-the-way sources. Their chief art consists in the happy selection of a Biblical passage to illustrate the subject chosen, and the ingenuity displayed in making the *cabalistica* count up correctly with as little alteration of the text as possible.

His *magnum opus*, which, as he tells us, cost him the labour of three whole days, was the *paragrammata* he constructed from Gen. xxxix. 2-33. He took the German pretty well as it came verse by verse, and absolutely made fourteen successive *cabalistica* out of it, each counting up 11,500, which was the number of a short account of Joseph which he took for his *programma*.

Riederer's preface is interesting for its simple-minded rambling account of his hobby, and how he defended it. He tells us that in 1714 he wished to send a little literary congratulation to a well-known professor at Altdorf, and at that time had not so much as heard what a *paragramma* was. However, while turning over the leaves of that amusing collection of literary trifles, *Das A.B.C. cum notis variorum*, 1703-8, he came across a wedding congratulation to a certain Matthew Walther and his bride, wherein their names were cleverly paragrammatised from the first two verses of Psalm xx.: " The Lord hear thee in the day of trouble ; the Name of the God of Jacob defend thee ; send thee help from the sanctuary, and strengthen thee out of Zion." This he thought most *apropos*. Possibly he remembered his own " day of trouble," and how he longed to be " strengthened " at the altar and the wedding festivals and through the honeymoon. Anyhow, it set him to work on his Bible, and in a few hours he produced an attempt which he considered very satisfactory. By practice he soon became a quicker workman, and sometimes, so he tells us, he made ten, twelve, or even fifteen *cabalistica* in a day.

The critics and learned heads laughed at his work, and even the ordinary man in the street looked down upon it as a puerile waste of time, but he felt he could afford to despise their scorn, and he gives the following reasons :—

" 1. If a man has a private hobby of his own which does no harm to any one, and pleasantly occupies his own time, why need he care for the sneers of the unsympathetic?

" 2. Besides this, the great majority of these carping critics could not do the thing half so well or so easily as he could, for his commercial education and practice had made him unusually quick at figures. So he retorts upon them the old fable of the Fox and the Grapes—' They call the grapes green and sour because they cannot reach unto them.'

" 3. They say it is a waste of time. But is this so, really? Let some of my fellow-citizens and despisers ask themselves what they will, perforce, have to answer without equivocation in that day when the searching question is put, 'How hast thou put thy talent to use?' Will not many have to say in that day, 'Lord! I have spent much time in drinking and carousing, and often by excess I have been as it were a fool and a madman. Lord! I have spent whole nights over cards and gambling. Lord! I have wasted my time in lewd company, talking and smoking, and even worse than that, often until the break of day.'

" But," says our Augsburg merchant, " whatever else I may have to confess before the great Searcher of Hearts, I can freely and gladly confess this : ' Lord! many are the wakeful nights I have passed, and when sleep came not, then did I arise and make my cabala. Lord! I have so learned Thy Bible by the searching out of fitting texts, that my soul hath oft been quickened therewith. Lord! for Thy loving-kindness and Thy mercy's sake, count these my greatest sins.'"

There is a direct simplicity and genuineness here which must needs make us like the man. Moreover, he spoke well of our countrywomen, for in his catalogued *paragrammata* he takes the text Job xlii. 15 for what he has to say cabalistically about the English fair ones, and that is: " And in all lands were no women found so fair." With such a foundation we should like to be able to see the edifice he raised to their honour, but unfortunately his catalogue of 1050 *paragrammata* only contains the suitable texts he chose and the subject, but not the resulting cabala, except in two instances, where he uses metrical hymns instead of Bible texts.

Our Augsburg citizen was evidently very conscientious and scrupulous as to the other sex. He does not tell us so, but it comes out when he has to deal cabalistically with fair and frail ones, as Lais and others. The Apocrypha is all he will allow to such, and then only in words of shame and reproach—*e.g.*, for Lais he chose Sirach xxiii. 26 : " She shall leave her memory to be cursed, and her reproach shall not be blotted out " (6237). And even Madame de Maintenon had to take a back seat with 1 Esdras iv. 30, 31 : " And taking the crown from the king's head and setting it upon her own head, she also struck the king with her left hand. And yet for all this the king gaped and gazed upon her with open mouth ; if she laughed upon him he laughed also ; but if she took any displeasure at him, the king was fain to flatter, that she might be reconciled to him again " (16,924). This is a clever selection, no doubt, but nothing that Riederer did can compare for difficulty and ingenuity with the Latin cabalistic soliloquies of the Capucin, Josephus Mazza de Castanea, who followed the Italian school and adhered to the ordinary numerical *gematria* in use in his day.

The number of authors who have dealt with this Biblical cabala is very small, as will appear by the short bibliography appended. It must not, however, be supposed that these names complete the list of cabalists. There are several exponents of this curious art who do not appear in my book at all, because they have never dealt specially with any Biblical text, and therefore have no claim to be included in the collection.

For instance, there is Joannes Ignatius Summa de Wlatislaw, who between 1684 and 1699 wrote six Latin works, some almost entirely cabalistical, and what is more, they were metrical as well. A good cabala is not easy to compose in any case, but when it has to be confined in the bonds of metre as well, it becomes doubly difficult.

Then there is a cabalistic life of Christ, written throughout in Latin leonine hexameters, each one counting up exactly 1706, which was the year it was written and published. It extends to 176 lines, and takes in all the principal events of our Saviour's life in due order. It was written by a Belgian village pastor who had been a university professor, and is, I should say, the most laborious and difficult work of the kind ever written. I only know of one copy, and have sought in vain for many years to procure another for my collection. However, I made a transcript when I first came across the book.

Then there is Benedictus Rocca, who in 1631, when there was a general assembly at Padua of all the abbots and high dignitaries connected with the famous Benedictine monastery of Monte Cassino, conceived the curious fancy that he would try to turn the name of every member of the assembly into an appropriate metrical cabala. He had only three days left before the event when the idea struck him, and so, as he tells us, he had to work very hard, or in his own rhetorical language : *Multiplici numerorum catena constricto per asperiora Pindi cacumina triduo mihi fuit incedendum.* However, the task was completed in time and published, and the sixty-four members of the council had each and all their laudatory cabala—an hexameter in every case, and generally very neat and appropriate—*e.g.* :

Pater Domnus Angelus è Bononia Casinensis Regii Abbas.   439

CAB. SIMPLEX.

Hinc Patriam, Nomenque dedit Sors præscia morum.   439

Another, perhaps even better—

Pater Domnus Leander à Placentia Abbas Casinensis.   382

CAB. SIMPLEX.

Purior Aoniis natat iste Leander in undis.   382

These three writers are the best of the " outsiders," but some very good *cabalistica* often occur on Flemish and German broadsheets. Among the Jesuits, Caspar Pfliger, of the Bohemian Province, and among the Hungarian Piarists, Benedictus ab Annunciatione B.V.M., respectively distinguished themselves ; and as late as the year 1767 an anonymous poet belonging to the abbey of Seligenstadt published a folio pamphlet (*penes me*) in honour of the Archbishop of Mentz, where eight *chrono-cabalistica* and 146 *cabalistica*, all metrical (hexameters), are employed to ring the changes in the peals of praise therein offered— each hexameter counting 1763, the year of the Archbishop's anniversary.

Finally, we must remember one great distinction between the old esoteric cabala and the new Latin *cabalistica* of the seventeenth and eighteenth centuries. These latter were written by ingenious religious men to fill up their spare time, or to devote it to the Virgin, as did San Juan y Bernedo ; and with one exception there is no thought or claim for inspiration or esoteric teaching, or even " wisdom." They were *tours de force* simply. The one exception was our friend the Lutheran expositor mentioned before, and who has a place of honour in the appendix.

Surely all cabalists, and, indeed, all persons who take even the slightest interest in the subject, must admit that here in this Lutheran *tour de force* is a most remarkable specimen of the mystic art. The *cabalistica* are all without a single exception most clear, significant, and appropriate, and we must remember that our author had no predecessors in this particular cabala with triangular numbers. He was the first who used this particular arithmetical progression for cabalistic purposes, and I think it may be said that he raised it, as did many of the earliest printers, to its highest perfection at one bound. No one who came after him could get anywhere near him in the admirable simplicity, continuity, and aptness of his cabalistic exposition of the Biblical number. It is evidently *the* most remarkable specimen of this particular device in all literature, and the longest. His treatment of Daniel's numbers, 1290 and 1335, which are taken together, is also very good and must rank as a good second.

This book is rare, and like the great majority of books cited here, is not in the British Museum, or Bodleian, or any English library that I know of. The author's name I have for the present withheld advisedly, as I wished to give my readers a little trial of cabalistic skill for their leisure moments. I found out, quite by a chance trial, that the correct name and title of the author is contained in the three words I have put in capitals in the fourth line from the end of his 2300 exposition, viz., *Michael filius dei*, who was the one who should rise up as God's witness and revelator in the last days. Our author makes no reference whatever to himself in connection with the above, but I fully believe that he knew that he was thus cabalistically numbered and marked out as *Michael filius dei*, and believed that God would reveal, and was revealing, His last secrets through His humble and devoted servant and spiritual son.

VETUS TESTAMENTUM CABALISTICUM

VETUS TESTAMENTUM CABALISTICUM

Gen. i. 2, 3.

"And the earth was without form, and void; and darkness was upon the face of the deep. And the Spirit of God moved upon the face of the waters. And God said, Let there be light : and there was light."

Per gematriam, all the Hebrew letters in the above count up to 3963 if the last sentence, " Let there be light : and there was light," be omitted. Now Elchanon Paulus, the converted Jew, makes a great Christian cabalistic proof out of this in the following manner :—

The Jewish mystical expounders took the verse to mean that in the period before the Mosaic dispensation all was without form and void, and that even during the next period, when Israel was under the Law, there was darkness, though the Spirit of God was with them, and that it would not be till the third period or dispensation should come—viz., the times of the Messiah—that there should be light.

So the cabalistic number 3963 shows, says Paulus, how long the world should wait for the coming of the Messiah.

But what does the last sentence teach us ? What says the cabala ?

Now, " Let there be light : and there was light," in Hebrew counts up to 470, which is the very number of the Hebrew sentence, " My Son, the Messiah, shall be born."

And so the Scripture seems to indicate clearly by this cabala that about the year of the world 3963, God would send His Son, the Messiah, to be born as the Light of the World.

This is undeniably a neat piece of work, and this method of

hoisting the Jews with their own petard was an ingenious, happy thought, and proved effective in converting several Rabbis and learned Jews when the ordinary Christian propagandist arguments would have been of no avail. The conversion of a Jew, especially a learned one, was thought much more of in those days than at present, and this was the case in England as well as abroad. There would be a public baptism, a great concourse to hear the sermon, and there would be very often a goodly sized pamphlet describing the antecedents and conversion of the baptised Jew. Several such have come down to us, and are preserved in the British Museum and elsewhere.

My copy of Elchanon Paulus originally belonged to the Jesuits of Vienna, and has been carefully annotated. The Jesuits and the learned world generally were always ready to help and befriend a learned Jew who had accepted Christ. Indeed, Polanco, the literary manager and editor of Ignatius Loyola's writings, was a Neo-Christian Jew, and a great friend of the Basque saint.

GEN. xxviii. 3, 4.*

Aber der allmächtige Gott seegne dich und mache dich fruchtbar und mehre dich dass du werdest ein Hauffen Voelcker und gebe dir den Seegen Abraham dir und deinem Saamen mit dir.   9177

CABALA TRIGONALIS.

Die aller Holdseeligste Kayserliche Gemahlin Frau Frau Elizabeth Christina eine gebohrne Printzessin von Braunschweig Wolffenbüttel.

9177

Europaische Fama, No. 177.

* This German Scriptural *cabala trigonalis* obtained considerable credit and applause at Vienna when it was first circulated in 1714, and many copies were afterwards printed. There was a great desire among all the subjects of Charles VI. that the Emperor should have male progeny to maintain the succession to the throne; and when shortly afterwards the Empress Elizabeth bore a son to the Emperor, this prophetical cabala was still more admired, as well as the one from Luc. i. 15 on the Emperor, which is quoted farther on in its place. This prophecy had the merit of fulfilment, which was more than a very good and famous anagram by a Jesuit succeeded in obtaining. The anagram was " Carolus Sextus Imperator = Uxor pariet tres masculos," which was certainly neat and deserved success, though it was unable to command it. The author of our Biblical cabala was J. F. Riederer, a merchant-poet of Nuremberg, who was a very prolific cabalist, as appears in the Bibliography.

GEN. xxviii. 17.

Hæc est Domus Dei et Porta
Cęli.   937 ■

PER CAB. ORD.

Pura et munda mater.   937
SAN JUAN, *of Bernedo.*

GEN. xxx. 22, 23, 24.*

Der Herr gedacht aber an Rahel
und erhöret Sie und machte Sie
fruchtbar. Da ward Sie schwanger
und gebar einen Sohn und sprach :
Gott hat meine Schmach von mir
genommen und hiess Ihn Joseph
und sprach : Der Herr wolle mir
noch einen Sohn darzu geben.

15,103

CABALA TRIGONALIS.

Die aller durchlauchtigste Fürstin
und Frau Frau Elizabeth Christina
aus dem Hertzoglichen Stamme zu
Braunschweig Wolffenbüttel, der
Regierenden Römischen Kayserlichen Majestät Herrn Herrn
Caroli Sexti Gemahlin.   15,103

GEN. xxxv. 16, 17, 18.

Da gebar Rahel und es kam sie
hart an über der Geburt; da es
Ihr aber so sauer ward in der
Geburt, sprach die Wehmutter zu
Ihr : Fürchte dich nicht denn
diesen Sohn wirst du auch haben,
da Ihr aber die Seel ausgieng dass
Sie sterben muste, hiess Sie Ihn
Benoni.   15,670

CABALA TRIGONALIS.

Charlotta   Christina   Sophia †
gebohrne Prinzessin von Braunschweig Lüneburg des Kron-
Prinzen Alexii Petrowizii von
Russland schöne Gemahlin starb
in Kindel-Bett den xxxi Octobris,
1715.   15,670

GEN. xlix. 10.

The Sceptre shall not depart from
Judah, nor a lawgiver from between
his feet, *until Shiloh come.*

PER GEMATRIAM HEBR.

Until Shiloh come.   462
Jesus Son of David.   462
ELCHANON PAULUS.

* This followed in due course the cabala on Luc. i. 36, 37, as soon as the Empress
was convalescent.
† This was the young wife of that ill-fated son of Peter the Great, whose con-
demnation and untimely death are so well known.

Num. vi. 24.

Benedicat Dominus et Custodiat te, ostendat faciem suam tibi.   1734

Per Cab. ord. sed Leoninam et Metricam.

Dux pie! Florescas per mutua lustra senescas

Est custos Dominus: Patrius iste sinus.   Summa, 1734.*

Num. xxiv. 17.

There shall come a Star out of Jacob, and *a Sceptre shall rise* out of Israel.

Per gematriam Hebr.

A Sceptre shall rise.   457

Jesus Son of David.   457

Elchanon Paulus.

Num. xxiv. 17.

Stella orta ex Jacob.   837

Per Cab. ord.

En pura nota maculæ.   837

San Juan.

Num. xxiv. 23.

Who shall live *when God doeth this?*

Per gematriam Hebr.

When God doeth this.   417

Jesus-God.   417

Deut. xxviii. 8.

Der Herr wird gebieten dem Seegen dass er mit dir sey in allem das du vorniṁest.   5047

Cabala Trigonalis.

Fredrich Augustus König in Pohlen und Churfürst zu Sachsen.   5047

D. Zipfel,

in *Europaische Fama.*

---

* 1734 was the year when the Franciscans of Düsseldorf issued a congratulatory address to Charles Philip, Elector of Bavaria, containing many chronograms of 1734, and the above Scriptural and metrical *cabalisticon.*

2 REG. vii. 9.

Dieser Tag ist ein Tag gutter Bottschafft. 2934

PARAGRAMMA TRIGONALE.*

Der Zwölffte Tag des Monats Maii, MDCCXIV. 2934
D. ZIPFEL,
in *Europaische Fama*, p. 161.

2 REG. ix. 17, 18.

Da sprach Joram : Nimb einen Reuter und sende Ihnen entgegen und sprich : Ists Friede ? Der Reuter reit hin Ihnen entgegen und sprach : So sagt der König : Ists Friede ? Jehu sprach : Was gehet dich der Friede an ? Wende dich hinter mich. 13,823

CABALA TRIGONALIS.

(*On the Peace Convention at Rastatt.*)
Die zwei anjetzt in Rastatt sich befindliche grosse Friedens plenipotentiarii nemlich Printz Eugenius, Käyserlicher General Lieutenant einer Seits, und Duc de Villars, Marschal de France anderer Seits.
13,823

3 REG. x. 18.

Thronus Salomonis. 948

PER. CAB. ORD.

Augustissima Maria. 948

1 CHRON. xii. 3.

Alle Aeltesten Israel kamen zum König gen Hebron und David machet einen Bund mit ihnen zu Hebron vor dem Herrn, und sie salbeten David zum König über Israel nach dem Wort dess Herrn durch Samuel. 12,650

CABALA TRIGONALIS.

Georg Ludewig König von Gross-Britanien, Franckreich und Irrland, Beschützer dess Glaubens und dess Heyl. Romischen Reiches Churfürst ; Hertzog zu Braunschweig und Lüneburg. 12,650
J. F. RIEDERER.

* This was made in celebration of the return of Frederick Augustus, King of Poland, to Saxony.

At p. 245 of the above-mentioned periodical some apologies and corrections are made : 1. The author was not the famed jurist D. Zipfel, of Leipzig, but Herr Joh. Heinr. Zipfel, of Plauen. 2. "Gutter" has a "t" too much, and "Zwölffte" an "f" too much. The editor then presents a new cabala by Zipfel (see Ps. xci. 11, 12).

JOB xv. 33.

Er wird abgerissen werden wie ein
unzeitige Trauben vom Wein-
stock.   5161

JOB xix. 25.

For I know that *my redeemer
liveth, and* that *he shall stand at
the latter day upon the earth.*

CABALA TRIGONALIS.

Ludovicus der Vierzehende König
in Franckreich biss daher bey-
genahmet der Grosse.   5161

PER GEMATRIAM HEBR.

My Redeemer liveth, and He shall
stand at the latter day upon the
earth.   939
Jesus Christ, Son of God, my
Redeemer liveth.   939

ELCHANON PAULUS.

PSALMORUM LIBER.

PSALM i. 3.

Erit		48
Tanquam Lignum		145
Quod Plantatum est		195
Secus Decursus		161
Aquarum, quod		133
Fructum suum		158
Dabit		34
In tempore suo		152
		1026

Et Folium	91
Ejus non	87
Defluet, et	90
omnia	46
Quæcunque	113
Faciet	42
Semper	68
Prosperabuntur	182
	719

CABALA SIMPLEX.

Illustriss. et	165
Reverendissimus	181
Franciscus	103
Sanctę Romanę	114
Ecclesiæ	58
Presbyter	102
Cardinalis Sacratus	174
Ferrariensis	129
	1026

D. Dñs	37
Franciscus	103
Sanctæ Romanæ	116
Ecclesiæ	58
Presbiter	102
Cardinalis	82
Sacratus	92
Ferrariensis	129
	719

J. B. SPADIUS.

Psalm i. 3.

Erit tanquam lignum, quod plantatum est secus decursus aquarum quod fructum suum dabit in tempore suo.   1026

Cabala Simplex.

Ludovicus Quartusdecimus Borbonicus Dei Gratia Francorum et Navarreorum Rex Christianissimus et pius.   1026

J. B. Spadius.

Psalm ii. 2.

The kings of the earth stand up and the rulers take counsel together, against the Lord, and *against his anointed*.

Per gematriam Hebr.

Against His Anointed.   464
Jesus, the Son of Jehovah.   464

Psalm iii. 6.

40   61   53   84
Non timebo millia populi
128   17
circumdantis me.

Cabala 383 Simplex.

154   66   81
Sterembergius Viennæ Obsessæ
82
Defensor.

Psalm viii. 5.

Gloria et honore coronasti eum Deus.   1572
Gloria et honore coronasti eum Domine.   1411

Per Cab. ord.

Magnificavit eum in conspectu Regum.   1572
O Sancte Ildephonse Mariæ Virginis ope nate.   1411

San Juan.

Psalm xvi. 11.

At thy right hand there are pleasures for evermore.   856

Per gematriam Hebr.

That is Jesus Christ, Son of God.   856

Elchanon Paulus.

Psalm xviii. 38.

45   97   47   49
Cadent subtus pedes meos.

Cabala 238 Simplex.

136   102
Innocentius Pontifex.
Vienna plausus.

PSALM xix. 10.	PER CAB. ORD.
En dulcior super mel et favum.	Mater Domini mei per te vivit Alphonse.
1444	1444
	SAN JUAN.

PSALM xx. 1, 2.	CABALA TRIGONALIS.*
Der Herr erhöre dich in der Noth, der Nahme des Gottes Jacob schütze dich. Er sende dir die Hülffe vom Heiligthum, und stärcke dich aus Sion. 9026	Herr Matthäus Walther Herr Braütigam. Jungfrau Euphrosina Sibylla gebohrne Tünzelin als Jungfrau Braut. 9026
	Das A.B.C.

PSALM xxi. 1, 2, 3.

1. The *king* shall joy in thy strength, O Lord ; and in thy salvation how greatly shall he rejoice !

2. *Thou hast given him his heart's desire*, and hast not withholden the request of his lips.

3. For thou preventest him with the blessings of goodness : thou settest a *crown* of pure gold on his head.

These verses were used in 1701 by a licensed or protected Jew (Schutz-Jude) in addressing a curious cabalistical congratulation to Frederick of Prussia, when he changed his title of Elector for that of King.

From the first verse he takes the Hebrew word for king (Meleck). This counts up as 90. He then shows that the Jewish word for Churfürst, or Elector, also equals 90, and so gets a double application of the verse.

---

* It was this wedding cabala that first induced Riederer to try his hand in the art (see Introduction).

From verse 2, in Hebrew—

Thou hast given him his heart's desire.   1731

also,

Frederick III. of Brandenburg (Hebrew).   1731

From verse 3—

Crown	679	} Hebrew.
Königsberg	679	}

From these calculations he brings out many flattering predictions, and finishes by obtaining from the first word of the title of the Psalm in Hebrew, Johann Sigismund; from the first and second words, Georg Wilhelm; and from the first three words, Wilhelm der Grosse.

Daniel Ernst Jablonski, the court preacher, wrote a pamphlet depreciating this cabalistic attempt, and compared it unfavourably with chronograms, quoting one of the latter—FrIDerICh I. KönIg Von PreVssen WIrDt gesaLbet Den XVIII. IanVarII—as much better. Court preachers in Prussia never seem to like Jews.

PSALM xxi. 1.	PER GEMATRIAM HEBR.	
The king shall joy in thy strength, O Lord; and *in thy salvation how greatly shall he rejoice!*	The king shall joy.	448
	The King, Messiah.	448
	In thy Salvation how greatly shall he rejoice!	912
	That is King, Messiah, Jesus, Son of David.	912
	ELCHANON PAULUS.	

PSALM xxii. 1.	PER GEMATRIAM HEBR.	
My God, my God, *why hast thou forsaken me?*	Why hast thou forsaken me?	614
	These are the words of Jesus.	614
	HACKSPAN,	
	De Cabala, p. 286.	

PSALM xxii. 16.

151   17   40   71
Circumdederunt me canes multi.

CABALA 279 SIMPLEX.

61   57   41   120
Vienna urbs anno MDCLXXXIII.
Vienna plausus.

PSALM xxii. 16.

They pierced my hands and my feet.   499

PER GEMATRIAM HEBR.

That is Jesus, Son of David.   499

PSALM xxii. 18.

And on my vesture did they cast lots.   829

PER GEMATRIAM HEBR.

That is the vesture of Jesus, Son of God.   829
ELCHANON PAULUS.

PSALM xxiv. 5, 6.

Accipiet benedictionem a Domino et misericordiam a Deo salutari suo, hæc est enim generatio quærentium Dominum.   932

CAB. PER NUM. MIN.

Ludovicus Quartusdecimus Borbonus Dei Gratia Francorum et Navarreorum Rex Christianissimus.   932
J. B. SPADIUS.

PSALM xxxvii. 31.

Lex Dei ejus in corde ipsius.
        1296

PER CAB. ORD.

B. Alphonse Præsul Magnæ Ecclesiæ Toletanæ.   1296
SAN JUAN.

PSALM xxxviii. 8.

93   50   24   127   50
Afflictus sum et humiliatus sum
        61
nimis.

CABALA 405 SIMPLEX.

94   29   109   50
Mahometes IV. Imperator Asiæque
        123
Tyrannus.
Vienna plausus.

PSALM xlv. 2.

Diffusa est gratia in labiis tuis.
1288

PER CAB. ORD.

O Innocens manibus, et mundo corde.
1288

SAN JUAN.

PSALM xlv. 6.

Thy throne, O God, is for ever and ever : the *sceptre of thy kingdom* is a right sceptre.

PER GEMATRIAM HEBR.

Sceptre of thy kingdom. 827
That is Jesus Christ, Son of David.
827

PSALM lii. 8.

Sicut Oliva fructifera in Domo Dei. 1373

Sicut Oliva fructifera. 1172

Oliva fructifera. 770

Oliva fructifera in Domo Dei plantata. 1294

In Domo Dei plantata. 524

Sicut Oliva fructifera in Domo Domini. 1497

PER CAB. ORD.

Ildephonsus infatigabilis Evangelii Prꜩco. 1373

Prꜩservata a macula originis. 1172
Prꜩstantissima Virgo Maria. 1172

Cœlum splendidum. 770

Maria præservata a macula originis.
1294

En Divina Mater. 524

Laudate eam cœtus Apostolorum.
1497

SAN JUAN.

PSALM lxiii. 3.

Labia mea laudabunt te in vitâ meâ.
1137

Macula remota est a Virgine piâ.
1137

PSALM lxviii. 16.

Mons in quo beneplacitum est Deo. 1308

En Cælum animatum sed Cꜩlo capacius. 1308

Psalm lxxi. 8, etc. (a cento).

Repleatur os meum laude tua;
nomen tuum vivet in æternum;
omnis terra repleta est gloria tua;
mirabilis Deus in sanctis suis.

5936

O immaculatæ Conceptionis eximie
Cultor B. Ildephonsus Præsul
Toletanus Gloria decusque Ponti-
ficum Iubar Stellaque Doctorum

5936

San Juan.

Psalm lxxii. 17.

Cabala Simplex.*

Benedicentur in eo
Omnes tribus terræ
Ac omnes gentes
Magnificabunt eum.
} 620

(1) Dñus Maphæus	128	(2) Sanctissimus	150
Sanctæ	57	D.D.	8
Romanæ	59	Urbanus	86
Ecclesiæ	58	Octavus	90
Cardinalis	82	Pontifex	97
Barberinus	99	Optimus	101
Florentinus	137	Maximus	88
	620		620

J. B. Spadius, Trimphus ab Urbano VIII.

Psalm lxxxv. 10.

Misericordia et veritas obviaverunt
sibi; justitia et pax osculatæ sunt.

3841

O Animarum Solatrix in mæroribus
Rubicunda Aurora fulgida, pur-
purea.

3841

* Cabala (1) as Cardinal; (2) as Pope.

CABALISTICA QUATUOR.

PSALM XXV. 12, 13.

Est	40
Homo, qui	88
Timet	61
Dominum	79
Anima	34
Ejus	50
In bonis	74
Demorabitur	114
	540

PSALM xcii. 12.

Et ut	60
Palma	37
Florebit	79
et	23
Sicut	66
Cedrus	64
Libani	43
Multiplicabitur	168
	540

PSALM lxxii. 9.

Coram	44
Illo	42
Procident	94
Æthiopes	85
Et inimici	85
Ejus	50
Terram	67
Lingent	73
	540

PSALM lxxii. 11.

Et adorabunt	99
Eum	35
Omnes	58
Reges	50
Terræ	61
Omnes	58
Gentes	64
Servient ei	115
	540

CABALA SIMPLEX.

D. Dominus	89
Franciscus	103
Sanctæ	57
Romanæ	59
Ecclesiæ	58
Cardinalis	82
Sacratus	92
	540

J. B. SPADIUS, *De F. Sacrato, S.R.E. Card.*

These cabalistic devices came into fashion in Italy about 1620. The name given to them was χρησμοὶ ἰσόψηφοι.

The above is a most ingenious one in its selection of Biblical texts all counting up the same number, and that number (540) the number of a man, the very cardinal to whose honour the work containing this cabala was dedicated and composed, and must have cost its author much time and trouble, but as to *tours de force*, J. B. Spadius was *capable de tout*; he made anagrams of several hexameter lines in length, all pure centos from Virgil.

PSALM xci. 11, 12.

Der Herr hat seinen Engeln befohlen über dir dass sie dich behüten auf allen deinen Wegen dass sie dich auf den Händen tragen und du deinen Fuss nicht an einen Stein stössest.   9818

PARAGRAMMA TRIGONALE.

Des Königlich - Polnischen und Chur-Printzens von Sachsen Hoheit befinden sich jetziger Zeit auf der Reise nach ausländischen Höffen und Provincen.   9818

J. H. ZIPFEL, *of Plauen.*

PSALM xcii. 12.

Justus ut Palma florebit.

CABALISTIC QUERY.

257   190   82   232
Ecquis ut Palma florebit?   761

CABALA ORD.

194   108   459
Quidam homo justus.   761

ANON.

Compare the Anagrammatic Query—

Quis est virtute præditus?

ANAGR.

Vir qui tutus et pars Dei est.

PSALM xcii. 12.

Justus ut Palma florebit; sicut Cedrus Libani multiplicabitur.

CABALA 624 MIN.

Jesu Deiparæ Virginis Mariæ Sponsus Sanctus JOSEPH Patriarcha.

ALONSO DE ALCALA.

Psalm xcii. 13.		Per Cab. ord.	
In Domo Dei plantata.	524	En Divina Mater.	524
		San Juan.	

Psalm xcvi. 1, 2.		Per Cab. Trig.	
Singet	540	Herr	357
dem Herren	566	Benjamin	369
ein neues Lied	789	Schmolck*	523
singet	540	Pastor	740
dem Herrn	551	Primarius	976
alle Welt	650	und	311
singet	540	Inspector	896
dem Herrn	551	der	178
und lobet	690	Evangelischen	790
seinen Namen	704	Kirchen	401
prediget	576	und	311
einen Tag	476	Schulen	595
am andern	440	zu	510
sein Heil	484	Schweidnitz	1140
	8097		8097

Psalm cx. 1.

The Lord said *unto my Lord, Sit thou at my right hand*, until I make thy enemies thy footstool.

Unto my Lord.	95
That is the Son of God.	95
Sit thou at my right hand.	452
Jesus, Son of David.	452

Psalm cx. 4.

The Lord hath sworn, and will not repent, *Thou art a priest* for ever after the order of Melchizedek.

Per gematriam Hebr.

Thou art a priest.	481
That is Jesus, Son of David.	481

Elchanon Paulus.

* Benjamin Schmolck was a famous hymn-writer. The above *Cab. Trig.* is from the Introduction to his *Sarten-Spiel des Hertzens*, Breslau, 1720, and is signed Joh. Fred. Riderer (*sic*).

PSALM cxviii. 21.

I will praise thee : for *thou* hast heard me, and *art become my salvation*.

PER GEMATRIAM HEBR.

Thou art become my salvation. 882
Jesus Christ, Son of God.
Jeschua Maschiach ben Elohim.
                              882

PSALM cxxviii. 5, and xx. 2.

Der Herr segne dich und stärcke dich aus Zion.   2899

PER CAB. TRIG.

Johann   George   Churfürste   zu
Sachsen.   2899
                    Das A.B.C.

PSALM cxxxii. 17.

There will I make the horn of David to bud.   839

PER GEMATRIAM HEBR.

Jesus, the King Messiah.   839
          ELCHANON PAULUS.

PSALM cxlviii. 1.

Laudate eam omnes populi.   981

PER CAB. ORD.

En non deturpata maculâ.   981

PSALM cxlviii. 2.

Laudate eam omnes angeli.   664

PER CAB. ORD.

En fælicissima Virgo.   664

PSALM cxlviii. 3.

Laudate eam Sol et Luna ; laudate eam omnes stellę et lumen.   2105

PER CAB. ORD.

Sponsa Spiritus Sancti, legitime
vocaris munda.   2105

PROV. i. 5, 6.

Wer Weise ist, der höret zu und bessert sich, und wer verständig ist, der lässet ihm rathen dass er vernehme die Sprüche und ihre Deutung, die Lehre die Weisen und ihre Beyspiel.   12,698

PER CAB. TRIG.

Herr Christian Weise, berühmter Rector des Gymnasii in Zittau, gebohren anno Christi 1642 den 30 April, und starb selig A. 1708 den 21 Octobr.   12,698

PROV. viii. 7, 8.

Veritatem meditabitur guttur meum, labia mea detestabuntur impium; justi sunt omnes sermones mei.

941

CAB. PER NUM. MIN.

Ludovicus Quartusdecimus Borbonius Dei Gratia Francorum et Navarreorum Rex Christianissimus.

941

J. B. SPADIUS.

PROV. viii. 20, 21.

In viis justitiæ ambulabo, ac in medio semitarum judicii, ut ditem diligentes me et thesauros eorum repleam.   931

CAB. PER NUM. MIN.

Ludovicus Quartusdecimus Borbonius Dei Gratia Gallorum et Navarreorum Rex Christianissimus.

931

J. B. SPADIUS.

PROV. viii. 35.

Whoso findeth me findeth life.   370

PER GEMATRIAM HEBR.

Ze Maschiach (That is Christ).   370

ELCHANON PAULUS.

PROV. viii. 36.

Illi * qui in me peccaverint lædent animam suam; omnes qui me oderunt, diligunt mortem.   741

CAB. PER NUM. MIN.

Ludovicus Quartusdecimus Borbonus, D. G. Galliæ ac Navarræ Rex Christianissimus.   741

J. B. SPADIUS.

PROV. ix. 1.

Sapientia Dei ędificavit sibi Domum.

1103

PER CAB. ORD.

Repleta Spiritu Sancto.   1103

SAN JUAN.

PROV. x. 6, 7, and 31.

Benedictio Domini super caput IVSTI, memoria ejus cum laudibus, ac os ejus parturiet sapientiam.

863

CAB. PER NUM. MIN.

Ludovicus Quartusdecimus Borbonius Dei Gratia Francorum ac Navarræ Rex Christianissimus. 863

J. B. SPADIUS.

* The Biblical text is in the singular number.

Prov. xx. 28.

Misericordia et veritas custodient
Regem et roborabitur clementia
thronus ipsius *.　　　　　　793

Cab. per num. min.

Ludovicus Quartusdecimus Borbonus, Gallorum et Navarræ Rex
Christianissimus.　　　　　　793

J. B. Spadius.

Prov. xxi. 1.

Cor Regis stat in manibus Domini
Dei et quocunque ipse voluerit
inclinabit illum.　　　　　　742

Cab. per num. min.

Ludovicus Quartusdecimus Borbonus, D. G. Galliæ ac Navarræ
Rex Christianissimus.　　　　742

J. B. Spadius.

Prov. xxx. 4.

Who hath ascended up into heaven,
or descended ?　Who hath gathered
the wind in his fists ?　Who hath
bound the waters in a garment ?
Who hath established all the ends
of the earth ?　What is his name,
and what is *his son's name*, if thou
canst tell ?

Per gematriam Hebr.

His son's name.　　　　　　398
That is Jesus (Ze Jeschua).　398

Elchanon Paulus.

Prov. xxxi. 20, 27.

$$\begin{array}{cccc} 301 & 321 & 464 & 168 \end{array}$$
Manum suam aperivit inopi
$$\begin{array}{ccccc} 105 & 136 & 300 & 130 & 201 \end{array}$$
Et panem otiosa non comedit.

2126

Per Cab. ord.

$$\begin{array}{cccc} 340 & 234 & 9 & 140 \end{array}$$
Christina　Borbonia　de　Francia
$$\begin{array}{cccc} 312 & 397 & 552 & 142 \end{array}$$
Sabaudie Ducissa Cypri Regina.

2126

Angelo Maria de Servatoribus.

Cant. ii. 2.

Lilium inter spinas.　　　731

Per Cab. ord.

Immunis a labe originis.　　731
Pura a mortali esca.　　　　731
Integra Deum parit.　　　　731

* Vulg., *ejus*.

CANT. iii. 7.

Lectulus Salomonis. 1018

PER CAB. ORD.

Mater et pietatis et clementiæ.
1018

Nubes luce refulgens. 1018

CANT. iv. 7.

Macula non est in te. 734

PER CAB. ORD.

Regina tota pura. 734

CANT. iv. 11.

Favus distillans labia ejus; mel et
lac sub lingua ejus. 2274

PER CAB. ORD.

Laudabilis et gloriosus Archipræsul
Ecclesiæ Toletanæ Primas His-
paniarum. 2274

CANT. iv. 12.

Hortus conclusus. 1179

PER CAB. ORD.

Nostra consolatrix. 1179

CANT. iv. 12.

Fons signatus. 723

PER CAB. ORD.

Mala nostra pelle. 723
En miraculum Magni Dei. 723
En immunis lue Adami. 723

(On the new-born heir to Charles VI.)*

CANT. v. 13, 14, 15.

Seine Lippen sind wie Rosen die
mit fliessenden Myrrhen trieffen:
seine Hände sind wie guldene
Ringe voll Türkissen: sein Leib
ist wie rein Elffenbein mit Sap-
phieren geschmückt: seine Beine
sind wie Marmel-Seulen gegründet
auf guldenen Füssen, seine Gestalt
ist wie Libanon auserwehlt wie
Cedern. 19,544

PARAGRAMMA CAB. TRIGONALE.

Der Durchlanchtigste Printz
Leopoldus Ertz - Hertzog zu
Oesterreich und Printz von
Asturien, Ihre Majestät des
Römischen Kaysers Caroli Sexti
und der Kayserin Elizabetha
Christina erstgebohrner Sohn,
gebohren den 13 April anno
Christi 1716. 19,544

J. F. RIEDERER.

* This much-looked-for little Prince with his "rosy lips" and "ivory skin"
was, alas! dead by November, and the praises and prognostications, anagrammatic,
cabalistic, and chronogrammatic, all fell to the ground. No Royal infant ever
received such a remarkable round of applause from all the workers in literary
ingenuities, as did this unfortunate Prince. I have enough material in my library
to fill a goodly volume.

CANT. vi. 4.

Ecce terribilis ut castrorum acies
ordinata. 1747

PER CAB. ORD.

Domus panis quem Diva coxit
Charitas. 1747

CANT. vi. 4.

Terribilis ut castrorum acies
ordinata. 1731

PER CAB. ORD.

Tu conscia omnium secretorum
Chti. 1731

CANT. vi. 4.

Ut castrorum acies ordinata. 1327

PER CAB. ORD.

Sancta Maria succurre miseris. 1327
SAN JUAN.

CANT. vi. 4.

Castrorum acies ordinata. 1027

PER CAB. ORD.

Speculum bonitatis Dei. 1027

CANT. vi. 10.

Sicut aurora consurgens. 1459

PER CAB. ORD.

Ecce totum mundum illuminans.
1459
O velox auscultatrix. 1459
Virgo prius ac posterius. 1459
SAN JUAN.

CANT. viii. 5.

Quæ est ista quæ ascendit ? 1199

PER CAB. ORD.

Portus Christianorum. 1199

ISA. vii. 14.

Behold a Virgin (Hebr. *Haalmah*)
shall conceive, and bear a son. 922

PER GEMATRIAM HEBR.

This same Virgin (*Haalmah*) is the
Virgin Mary. 922

ISA. vii. 14.

And she shall call his name
Immanuel.   1250

PER GEMATRIAM HEBR.

His name is Jesus Christ, the Son
of God.   1250

ISA. ix. 6.

For unto us a child is born, unto
us a son is given.   812

His name is Wonderful.   457

Wonderful, Counsellor, Mighty
God.   529

PER GEMATRIAM HEBR.

Jesus is born unto us from Maria.
                             812

Jesus, son of David.   457

Jesus, son of God.   529
             ELCHANON PAULUS.

ISA. ix. 6.

Admirabile est tuum nomen. 1051

PER CAB. ORD.

Lampas inextinguibilis.   1051
                    SAN JUAN.

ISA. xi. 1.

And there shall come forth a rod
out of the stem of Jesse, and *a
Branch shall grow out of his roots.*

PER GEMATRIAM HEBR.

Out of the stem of Jesse.   440
The Virgin Mary (Haalmah
Miream).   440
A Branch shall grow out of his
roots.   1497
Jesus of Nazareth, the Messiah, is
out of Mary.   1497

ISA. xi. 2.

Requievit super eum Spiritus
Sapientiæ.   2136

PER CAB. ORD.

Ecce purissimæ Conceptionis B.
Virginis eximiè cultor.   2136
                    SAN JUAN.

Isa. xi. 10.

And in that day *there shall be a root of Jesse*, which shall stand for an ensign of the people ; to it shall the Gentiles seek : and *his rest shall be glorious.*

PER GEMATRIAM HEBR.

There shall be a root of Jesse. 1146
Jesus Christ shall be out of Jesse.
                                    1146
His rest shall be glorious.   536
That is Jesus, Son of God.   536

Elchanon Paulus here also makes use of Notaricon, the cabala of initials and finals. Taking the consecutive initials of the fifteen Hebrew words which are contained in Isa. xi. 10, he gets : *Ke ba Jeschua hagoel am*, which he renders "Then comes Jesus, the Redeemer of the Nations." Taking the finals, he gets : *Im sod hod schemimiriom—i.e.*, "That is the mystery of the honour which shall come to Mary."

N.B.—I give Elchanon's own transliteration of the Hebrew in all the instances I quote. I believe that throughout his book his *gematria* or counting up is accurate, but he occasionally indulges in the licence of changing a vowel or reduplicating a letter.

Isa. xiii. 11.

$\overset{98}{\text{Quiescere}}$ $\overset{32}{\text{faciam}}$ $\overset{99}{\text{superbiam}}$
$\overset{98}{\text{infidelium.}}$

$\overset{24}{\text{Et}}$ $\overset{111}{\text{arrogantiam}}$ $\overset{97}{\text{fortium}}$ $\overset{86}{\text{humiliabo.}}$

PER CAB. SIMP. 327.

$\overset{73}{\text{Joannes}}$ $\overset{129}{\text{Subieskius}}$ $\overset{82}{\text{Poloniæ}}$ $\overset{43}{\text{Rex.}}$

PER CAB. SIMP. 318.

$\overset{84}{\text{Carolus}}$ $\overset{45}{\text{Dux}}$ $\overset{189}{\text{Lotaryngyensis.}}$
                              Vienna plausus.

Isa. xxxii. 1.

Behold a king shall reign in righteousness.   469

PER GEMATRIAM HEBR.

Jesus, Son of God.   469

Isa. xli. 11.

Sihe, sie sollen zu Spott und zu Schanden werden Alle, die dir gram sind, sie sollen werden als nichts, und die Leut so mit dir hadern sollen umkommen.   10,287

PER CAB. TRIG.

Herr Doctor Philipp Jacob Spener, anfänglich des venerandi Ministerii in Franckfurth Senior, hernach Probst, Inspector und Consistorial-Rath in Berlin.   10,287

Isa. xlii. 1.

Behold my servant, whom I up-
hold ; mine elect. 840

Per gematriam Hebr.

That is Jesus Christ, Son of God.
840
Elchanon Paulus.

Isa. lii. 13.

Behold, my servant shall deal
prudently, he shall be exalted and
extolled, and be very high.

Per gematriam Hebr.

Behold, my servant shall deal
prudently, he shall be exalted. 772
That is Jesus Christ. 772

Isa. lxi. 1.

He hath sent me to bind up the
broken-hearted, to proclaim liberty
to the captives, etc.

Per gematriam Hebr.

He hath sent me. 398
That is Jesus (Ze Jeschua). 398

Isa. lxii. 2.

Du sollst	818
mit einem	557
neuen Namen	685
genennet	536
werden	515
	3111
Jahrzahl	1714
Zahl des Tages an welchen die erste Proclamation in Engelland geschehen viz. 12 Aug.	224
	5049

Per Cab. Trig.

Georgius	755
Ludovicus	1033
Churfürst	1150
zu	510
Braunschweig	990
Hanover	611

(N.B.—George I.
proclaimed King
of England, Aug.
12, 1714.)

5049
J. F. Riederer.

4

Isa. lxii. 3.		Per Cab. Trig.	
Du	220	Georg	329 ·
wirst sein	1343	Ludewig	650
eine schöne	590	Churfürst	1150
Crone	370	zu	510
in der Hand	452	Braunschweig	990
des Herrn	644	Hanover	611
und ein	462	wird	394
Königlicher Hut	1081	auf den Thron	923
in der Hand	452	von Engelland	789
deines Gottes	1046	erhaben	314
	6660		6660

J. F. Riederer.

Jer. xxiii. 5.

Behold, the days come, saith the Lord, that I will raise *unto David a righteous Branch*, and a King shall reign and prosper.

Per gematriam Hebr.

Unto David a righteous Branch.
386

Jesus. 386

Elchanon Paulus.

Jer. xxxi. 22.

En mulier circumdans virum. 1338

Per Cab. ord.

En Maria preservata a macula originis. 1338

En aurora lucida et rubicunda.
1338

Lęva Sponsi sub capite ejus. 1338

San Juan.

Ezek. xxxvii. 25.

And my servant David shall be their prince. 544

Per gematriam Hebr.

Jesus, the Son of David, the King.
544

Elchanon Paulus.

EZEK. xliv. 2.

Porta clausa. 606

Porta mirè clausa. 730

PER CAB. ORD.

Spes nostra. 606
Liberatrix. 606
Immunis labe originis. 730
Pura mortali esca. 730
Agna vera mira munda. 730
Nitida et pura Maria. 730

SAN JUAN.

DAN. ii. 34.

Petra a montis vertice abscissa. 852

PER CAB. ORD.

Maria Virginea et munda. 852

SAN JUAN.

DAN. vii. 13.

I saw in the night visions, and, behold, *one like the Son of man came* with the clouds of heaven.

PER GEMATRIAM HEBR.

One like the Son of man came. 995
That is Jesus Christ, Son of God (Ze hu Jeschua Maschiach bar El). 995

DAN. vii. 25, 26.

Er wird den Höchsten lästern, und die Heiligen des Höchsten verstören, und wird sich unterstehen Zeit und Gesetze zu ändern; sie werden aber in seine Hand gegeben werden eine Zeit und etliche Zeit und eine halbe Zeit; darnach wird das Gericht gehalten werden; da wird dann seine Gewalt weggenommen werden, dass er zu Grund vertilget und umbracht werde.

23,403

PER CABALAM TRIGONALEM.*

Das in ein-tausend sieben-hundert und achtzehenden Jahr nach der gnadenreichen Geburt JESV Christi zu grund gehen und wo nicht völlig per terram gestürtzte, doch durch das Aller-Durchleuchtigste Hauss Oesterreich und dessen Grossmachtigstes Ober-Haubt in das aller empfindlichste Abnehmen und Confusion gebrachte Mahometanische oder Türkische Reich.

23,403

MICAH iv. 1.

Domus Domini in vertice montium.
1326

Mons in vertice montium. 1120

PER CAB. ORD.

Reparatrix naturę humanę. 1326

O salus in te sperantium. 1120

* This cabalistical prognostication appeared in Anton Fabri's *Europäischer Staats-Kantzlei* (part 30, p. 514), 1718. 8. Riederer was the author, as he tells us in his *Catalogues*.

Micah v. 2, 3.

But thou, Beth-lehem Ephratah, though thou be little among the thousands of Judah, yet out of thee shall he come forth unto me *that is to be ruler in Israel*; whose goings forth have been from of old, from everlasting. *Therefore will he give them up, until the time that she which travaileth hath brought forth.*

Per gematriam Hebr.

That is to be ruler in Israel.   919
Jesus Christ, King of the Jews.   919
Therefore will he give them up, until the time that she which travaileth hath brought forth.   1248
That is at the very time when Jesus shall be born of Mary.   1248

Elcnanon Paulus.

Micah v. 4.

And he shall stand and *feed in the strength of the Lord.*

Per gematriam Hebr.

And he shall feed in the strength of the Lord.   386
Jesus (Jeschua).   386

Micah v. 9.

125	64	40	75
Exaltabitur	manus	tua	super

82	71	
hostes	tuos.	457

Per Cab. Simpl.

138	151	62
Hippolytus	Centurionus	Heros

106	
Januensis.*	457

Habac. iii. 3.

Venit ab Austro Deus.   1177

Per Cab. ord. 1177.

1. Id a Deo ; Archidux Leopoldus.
2. Erit Leopoldus ab Austria.
3. Filius primogenitus Caroli.
4. Filius Caroli Sexti hic dimicat.
5. Ille Leopoldus e Domo Austriacâ.
6. Ab ea donatus in Die Deci-
matertia Aprilis.

---

* This appropriate numerical anagram refers to a famous incident in the war against the Turks (1683). The hero of the cabala, a Genoese of noble birth, having command of a single ship only, fell in with a fleet of forty-six Turkish triremes. He fought obstinately against capture, and eventually escaped with his ship, although he was badly wounded, and had his left hand struck off in the fight. See another on him, Baruch iii. 5.

The cabala is the simple one—$a = 1$; $b = 2$; . . . $z = 23$.

These six Scriptural *cabalistica* had their origin from the following historical event:—

On April 13th, 1716, there was born to the Emperor Charles VI. and his Consort, Elisabeth Christina, a long-desired son, who was baptised as Leopoldus Joannes Josephus Antonius Franciscus de Paula Hermenegildus Rudolphus Ignatius Balthasar.

The birth of this heir to the Imperial Throne brought forth acclamations from all quarters, and the number of anagrams, chronograms, and *cabalistica* made in honour of the happy event is remarkably large.

I have a large folio volume of several hundred pages, published at Prague in 1716, containing the laudatory contributions of the Jesuits of the Province of Bohemia alone. Here there are 593 chronograms of the year of birth (1716), and various *cabalistica* and anagrams besides. And there are several other similar productions. But in spite of all the good omens and hopes, the infant died on November 4th in the same year (1716), or, as it was neatly expressed chronogrammatically—

$$\left.\begin{array}{l}\text{In hoCCe anno} \\ \text{DIe qVartà noVeMbrIs} \\ \text{Infans obIIt}\end{array}\right\} = 1716$$

his birth being cabalistically expressed with equal skill thus :—

Hic Leopoldus enatus in Mense Aprilis et ad Pascha.   1716

The Scriptural cabala here quoted are from a MS. (*penes me*) entitled : "Mysterium Magnum in auspicatissimo Natali Serenissimi Austriæ Archiducis Asturiæque Principis Leopoldi revelatum.   Oratio Pythagorica."

Hab. iii. 13.	Per gematriam Hebr.
Thou wentest forth for the salvation of thy people, even *for salvation with thine anointed.*	For salvation with thy Messiah.
	1189
	That is with Jesus thy Messiah.
	1189
	Elchanon Paulus.

ZECH. xii. 8.

And the house of David shall be as God. 548

PER GEMATRIAM HEBR.

That is Jesus, the Son of God. 548
ELCHANON PAULUS.

ZECH. iv. 7.

Who art thou, O great mountain? before Zerubbabel thou shalt become a plain : and he shall bring forth *the headstone* thereof with shoutings, crying, Grace, grace unto it.

PER GEMATRIAM HEBR.

The Headstone. 569
That is Jesus, Son of King David. 569
ELCHANON PAULUS.

ZECH. ix. 9.

Rejoice greatly, O daughter of Zion ; shout, O daughter of Jerusalem : behold, *thy King cometh unto thee: he is just, and having salvation* ; lowly, and riding upon an ass.

PER GEMATRIAM HEBR.

Thy King cometh unto thee : he is just, and having salvation. 815
Jesus Christ, Son of David (Jeschuah Maschiach ben David). 815
ELCHANON PAULUS.

ZECH. vi. 12.

Behold the man whose name is The BRANCH. 855

PER GEMATRIAM HEBR.

That is Jesus Christ, the Son of God (Ze hu Jeschuah hamaschiach ben El). 855

Also another cabalistical identity—

The Branch (Hebr. *Zemach*). 138

The Son of God (Hebr. *Ben Elohim*). 138
ELCHANON PAULUS.

APOCRYPHA

APOCRYPHA

1 Esdras iv. 3, 4, 7, 8.

Aber der König bezwinget sie alle, als der über sie herrschet und alles was er ihnen gebietet das thun sie. Sie erwürgen und werden erwürget, und des Königes Worte gehen sie nit vorbei, heist er töden so töden sie, heist ers nachlassen so lassen sie es heist er zuschlagen so schlagen sie.   19,964

Per Cab. Trig.

Serenissimus et Potentissimus Dominus Tzarus Petrus Alexiovicius Magnus Dux totius magnæ, parvæ, et albæ Russiæ autocrator, Moscoviæ, Cyoviæ, Volodomiriæ, Novogardiæ aliorumque Dominus ac totius Septentrionalis Oræ Dominator, etc.   19,964

J. F. Riederer.

2 Esdras xi. 37.

42 16 78 30 9 59
Vidi ecce sicuti Leo de Silva
119   89   95
concitatus rugiens demittebat
54 5 70
ocem ad aquilam.   666

Cabala Simplex.

112   96   108
Leopoldus Ignatius Franciscus
88   69   95
Baltassar Joseph Felicianus
93   4 1
Maximus D. A.   666

Albricius, Nicolas.*

* See Bibliography.

JUDITH iii. 1-6.

Da schickten sie ihre Bottschafften aus, die kamen zu ihm und sprachen, wende deinen Zorn von uns denn es ist besser dass wir dem grossen König deinen und dir gehorsam seyn und lebendig bleiben, denn dass wir umbkommen und gewennen gleichwohl nichts, alle unsere Städte, Güter Berge, Hügel Aecker, Ochsen, Schaafe, Ziegen, Rosse und Cameel und was wir nun haben ; darzu auch unser Gesind ist alles dein, schaffe damit was du wilt, ja auch wir samt unsern Kindern sind deine Knechte, kom zu uns und sey unser gnädiger Herr und branche unsers Diensts wie dirs gefället. 37,457

PER CAB. TRIG.

Das gedemüthigte und sich submittirende Belgrad oder Griechisch Weisenburg in Servien an der Donau olmferne dem San Fluss gelegen, aus der Türckischen Hunde Händen gerissen und per accord den achtzehenden Augusti anno ein Tausend siebenhundert und siebenzehen an die Kayserliche Waffen siegreiche übergangen unter glücklichen Commando des durchlauchtigsten Generalissimi Printzen Eugenii Francisci Hertzogen von Savoyen und Piemont, Marggraffen zu Saluces, Rittern des güldenen Vlieses und bey Ihren Kayserlichen Majestät Hof-Kriegs-Rath Præsidenten. 37,457

J. F. RIEDERER.

SAP. v. 18, 19.

Induet pro thorace justitiam, accipiet pro galea judicium certum, sumet scutum inexpugnabile æquitatem. 953

CAB. PER NUM. MIN.

Ludovicus Quartusdecimus Borbonicus, Dei Gratia Francorum et Navarrensium Rex Christianissimus. 953

J. B. SPADIUS.

SAP. x. 10.

IVSTVM deduxit Dominus per vias rectas, et ostendit illi regnum Dei ; honestavit illum in laboribus, et complevit labores illius. 1195

CAB. PER NUM. MIN.

Ludovicus Tertiusdecimus Borbonicus, Dei Gratia Francorum et Navarrensium Rex Christianissimus, cognomentoque Iustus. 1195

J. B. SPADIUS.

Sap. xii. 15-19.

Weil du denn gerecht bist so regierest du alle Dinge recht, und achtest deiner Mäjestät nicht gemäss jemand zu verdammen, der die Straffe nicht verdienet hat. Denn deine Stärcke ist eine Herrschaft der Gerechtigkeit und weil du über alle herrschest so verschonest du auch aller. Denn du hast deine Stärcke beweiset, an denen so nicht glaubeten dass du so gar mächtig wärest, und hast dich erzeiget an denen die sich keck wusten. Aber du gewaltiger Herrscher richtest mit Lindigkeit und regierest mit viel verschonen denn du vermagst alles was du wilt. Dein Volck aber lehrest du durch solche Werck dass man fromm und gütig seyn solle. 41,332

Per Cab. Trig.

Der Durchleuchtigste Grossmächtigste Fürst und Herr, Herr Friederich Augustus erwehlter König in Pohlen, Gross Herzog in Litthauen, Reussen, Preussen, Mazovien, Samogitien, Kyovien, Wolhynien, Podolien, Podlachien, Lieffland, Smolenskien, Severien und Schernicovien; Herzog zu Sachsen Jülich, Cleve, Berg, Engern und Westphalen, des Heiligen Römischen Reichs Erz-Marschall und Churfürst, Landgraf in Thüringen, Marckgraf zu Meissen auch Ober und Nieder Lausitz, Burggraf zu Magdeburg, Gefürsteter Graf zu Henneberg, Graf zu der Marck Ravensberg und Barby, Herr zum Ravenstein.* 41,332

J. F. Riederer.

---

* The prolonged accumulation of titles is not uncommon in either literal or numerical anagrams, but we seldom meet such an enormous specimen as the above. However, in 1705, G. Gothofredus produced a pure literal anagram of somewhat similar length on the same king. I quote it in text (although non-Biblical) for the purpose of comparison. Which of the two would take the longer time to compose, I can hardly say; I think the literal anagram, but both are unique of their kind.

Prose anagrams of such a length as 567 letters are very seldom met with. I only know four that surpass the above in length and ingenuity. One of the best, though not quite the longest, is the prose anagram of 1072 letters made out of Psalm xc., and addressed to the Emperor Leopold in 1684. This, being a Biblical anagram, will appear in my *Biblia Anagrammatica*. But the greatest anagrammatic curios are the metrical ones, which are very difficult to compose. I am acquainted with fifteen of

PROGRAMMA.

Dominus Friedericus Augustus Potentissimus Poloniarum Rex, Magnus Dux Lithuaniæ, tum Russiæ ac Prussiæ, Masoviæq, tum Samogitiæ, tum Vollhiniæ ac Podoliæ, tum Podlachiæ, tum Livoniæ, porro et Smolensciæ, tum Severiæ, sicut et Czernikoviæ; adhæc et Dux Saxoniæ Juliaci simul et Cliviæ, et Montium, pariterque Angariæ et Westphaliæ: quin et Sacri Romani Imperii Archi-Marschallus atque Elector, Landgravius insuper Thuringiæ, Marchio Misniæ, ut et tam superioris quam inferioris Lusatiæ, Burggravius Magdeburgensis, ac Princeps-Comes Hennebergensis, Comes pariter Marcæ, sic et Ravensburgæ atque Barby, Dominus Ravensteinii.

ANAGRAMMA PURISSIMUM.

Ecce hic est Rex Sarmatiæ verè legitimus! Quid STANISLAVS? Est perduellis. Ubi PRIMAS Regni, perduellium CARDINALIS? Mortuus. Rex noster autem vivat, Heros hic Mavortius, qui armatas hostium phalangas animo aggreditur intrepido! Vivat ejus amicus, ac armorum jam socius, Heros PETRVS ALEXIOWIZIVS Bene fiet SMIEGIELSKYO, qui Regi suo fidus? Bene omni Sarmatiæ, qui ab execrandâ ac iniquiori læsæ Majestatis crimine aggravatâ perduellione abhorrens, acclamat, pièque apprecatur. Vivat! benè vireat hic verè, hicce legitime unctus! Imo omnes universæ Sarmatiæ ditiones hunc verum Regem suum spontaneô, politiori, nec inani agnoscant applausu! FIAT!

[567 letters.]

these, all having more that six hundred letters. Some are written in musical monkish metres of nearly forty lines, and one (*facile princeps*) runs to the extraordinary length of 132 hexameter and pentameter lines, and contains 4419 letters. It is Casimir's hymn, *Omni die, die Mariæ,* finely turned into classic elegiacs. It is by a Jesuit of Prague, and was written *c.* 1672. There is a copy of the book containing it to be seen at the Prague University Library, but nowhere else, as far as I know. I transcribed it when at Prague some years ago, and shall place it in an anagrammatic Breviary if I get the opportunity of arranging and printing what I have.

ECCLI. xxiv. 2, etc.

In medio	63
Ecclesiæ	58
Aperiet	68
Os ejus,	80
Et implebit	111
Eum Dominus	110
Spiritu Sapientiæ	184
Et Intellectus,	149
Stolaque gloriæ	159
Induet eum	92
	1074

CABALA SIMPLEX.

Illustriss. atque	200
Reverendiss.	125
Dominus Dominus	170
Franciscus	103
Sanctæ	57
Romanæ	59
Ecclesię	57
Cardinalis	82
Sacratus	92
Ferrariensis	129
	1074

J. B. SPADIUS.

ECCLI. xxiv. 9.

Dominus tecum ab initio et ante secula. 1551

PER CAB. ORD.

O Regina cui se cœlum et terra subjicit. 1551

SAN JUAN.

ECCLI. xxiv. 13.

Sicut cedrus exaltata. 1312

PER CAB. ORD.

O Lilium in quo cubat Deus. 1312

SAN JUAN.

ECCLI. xxiv. 13.

Quasi Cypressus exaltata. 1435
En quasi Cypressus exaltata. 1480

PER CAB. ORD.

Stella ex qua Sol enituit. 1435
Jacobi Scala per quam ad Coelum ascenditur. 1480

SAN JUAN.

ECCLI. xxiv. 14.

Quasi Palma exaltata in Cades. 1162

PER CAB. ORD.

Jucundissima Virgo Maria. 1162

SAN JUAN.

ECCLI. xxiv. 14.

O quasi Palma exaltata. 1060

PER CAB. ORD.

Munda ex maculâ originali. 1060

SAN JUAN.

ECCLI. xxiv. 15.

Ich bin aufgewachsen wie Ahörnen, ich gab einen lieblichen Geruch von mir wie Cynnamet und köstliche Würze und wie die besten Myrrhen wie Galban und Onych und Myrrhen und wie der Weyrauch in dem Tempel.   13,486

PER CAB. TRIG.

Christian Hoffmann von Hoffmannswaldau auff Arnoldsmühl, der Römischen Kayserlichen Majestät Rath, wie auch Raths-Præses der Stadt Breslau, starb Anno Christi MDCLXXIX den xviii April.   13,486

J. F. REIDERER.

ECCLI. xxx. 4.

Mortuus est Pater ejus, sed quasi non est mortuus, similem enim reliquit sibi post se.   872

CAB. PER NUM. MIN.

Ludovicus Quartusdecimus Borbonius, Dei Gratia Gallorum et Navarræ Rex Christianissimus. 872

J. B. SPADIUS.

ECCLI. xxx. 6.

Pater ejus reliquit defensorem mirum Domus suæ contra inimicos, et amicis reddentem gratiam.   832

CAB. PER NUM. MIN.

Ludovicus Quartusdecimus Borbonicus, Dei Gratia Galliæ et Navarrę Rex Christianissimus. 832

J. B. SPADIUS.

ECCLI. xlv. 7.

Induit eum Dominus stolam gloriæ.   1483

PER CAB. ORD.

Ecce Alphonsus Præsul Ecclesiæ Toletanæ.   1483

SAN JUAN.

ECCLI. xlvii. 6.

Dedit illi Dominus coronam gloriæ.   1130

PER CAB. ORD.

Archiepiscopus Ecclesiæ Toletanæ.   1130

Theologorum Theologus.   1130

SAN JUAN.

Baruch iii. 5.

80   64   44 24   88
Memento manus tuę et nominis
48 23   87   60
tui in tempore isto.

Cabala 518 Simplex.*

151   151   39
Hyppolytus Centurionus, Tu
115   62.
Inclytus Heros.
Vienna plausus.

1 Machab. iv. 58.†

105 111 195   245   300 49 440   79   230
Et facta est Lætitia toto in populo magna valdè.   1754

1 Machab. viii. 14.

Und wurden sehr mächtig und
wan solche Tugend bey Ihnen dass
sich keiner zum König machte.
6043

Per Cab. Trig.
(*On the Dutch.*)

Die durch gantz Europa berühm-
ten Herrn Generaal Staaten der
vereinigten Provinzien.   6043
J. F. Riederer.

---

* See Micah v. 9, for another.

† This, which was called a *scripturistico-cabalisticon*, was exhibited at the election of a new Archbishop at Trèves in 1754, among other literary devices of the Jesuits there.

NOVUM TESTAMENTUM CABALISTICUM

NOVUM TESTAMENTUM CABALISTICUM

My New Testament collection begins with a long cabalistic soliloquy of the Virgin Mary on the words of the angel in Joseph's dream (Matt. ii. 13), "Flee into Egypt."

It comes from the remarkable book of Josephus Mazza, the laborious Capucin, a work so rare that I know of no other copies in England but my own. He uses the Vulgate for the texts of the soliloquies, and other texts will be found further on in St. Luke and St. John. Each soliloquy of the Virgin contains sixty-three cabala, that being her supposed age when she died. The wording is generally very appropriate, and the labour entailed in making such excellent cabalistic lines must have been enormous.

MATT. ii. 13.

SOLILOQUIUM.

$\overset{118}{\text{FUGE}}$ $\overset{39}{\text{IN}}$ $\overset{572}{\text{ÆGYPTUM.}}$ 729

1. $\overset{50}{\text{Hinc}}$ $\overset{470}{\text{exulandum}}$ $\overset{175}{\text{est}}$ $\overset{34}{\text{Filj}}$;   729

2. $\overset{95}{\text{Et}}$ $\overset{253}{\text{effugium}}$ $\overset{100}{\text{non}}$ $\overset{128}{\text{nisi}}$ $\overset{39}{\text{in}}$ $\overset{114}{\text{fuga}}$;   729

3. $\overset{104}{\text{Modò}}$ $\overset{1}{\text{à}}$ $\overset{159}{\text{Jordane}}$ $\overset{291}{\text{pergendum}}$ $\overset{5}{\text{àd}}$ $\overset{169}{\text{Nilum,}}$ 729

4. Et ibi Bethlem in Meroem immutanda.   729
$\overset{95}{} \overset{20}{} \overset{140}{} \overset{39}{} \overset{160}{} \overset{275}{}$

5. Quàm ergò execrandi Hebrei !   729
$\overset{181}{} \overset{122}{} \overset{327}{} \overset{99}{}$

6. Quàm impia hodiè, ac infanda Hierusalem !   729
$\overset{181}{} \overset{89}{} \overset{66}{} \overset{4}{} \overset{81}{} \overset{308}{}$

7. Si tàm deteriores Niliacis,   729
$\overset{89}{} \overset{111}{} \overset{378}{} \overset{151}{}$

8. Si impij sìc Cœli ardent in Numen,   729
$\overset{89}{} \overset{97}{} \overset{92}{} \overset{27}{} \overset{200}{} \overset{39}{} \overset{185}{}$

9. Tantum abs Dei Numine defecere,   729
$\overset{331}{} \overset{83}{} \overset{18}{} \overset{194}{} \overset{103}{}$

10. Jàmquè fiunt sic indè odibiles ;   729
$\overset{195}{} \overset{235}{} \overset{92}{} \overset{48}{} \overset{159}{}$

11. Ut modò ab eis aufugiens,   729
$\overset{190}{} \overset{104}{} \overset{3}{} \overset{94}{} \overset{338}{}$

12. Ad illosquè ità confugiens,   729
$\overset{5}{} \overset{314}{} \overset{100}{} \overset{310}{}$

13. Jàm perhorreas, deseras Jacob,   729
$\overset{30}{} \overset{399}{} \overset{245}{} \overset{55}{}$

14. Jàmquè diligas, & præferas Cham.   729
$\overset{195}{} \overset{120}{} \overset{95}{} \overset{287}{} \overset{32}{}$

15. Nèc quod jàm agis, immeritò agis,   729
$\overset{38}{} \overset{204}{} \overset{30}{} \overset{97}{} \overset{263}{} \overset{97}{}$

16. Hic barbarè ab Herode addictus es neci,   729
$\overset{20}{} \overset{151}{} \overset{3}{} \overset{132}{} \overset{291}{} \overset{85}{} \overset{47}{}$

17. At Chamitæ Tè recipient, alent ;   729
$\overset{91}{} \overset{136}{} \overset{95}{} \overset{271}{} \overset{136}{}$

18. Hic depulsus à Tuis,   729
$\overset{20}{} \overset{429}{} \overset{1}{} \overset{279}{}$

19. Ibi fies, eris, alienis dilectus.   729
$\overset{20}{} \overset{100}{} \overset{164}{} \overset{144}{} \overset{301}{}$

20. Hinc illic non Tui, Tui fient.   729
$\overset{50}{} \overset{41}{} \overset{100}{} \overset{199}{} \overset{199}{} \overset{140}{}$

21. Et ab indè amodò Ecclesia erit in Semine.   729

      95 3 48   105   116   174 39   149

22. Ad hæc læta mi Filj tandèm mè benè deduxi.   729

      5 16 106 29 34   150   25   42   322

23. Ut ægrum ego foveam Cor :   729

      190 202   52   172   113

24. Ut audij mandatum Cœli dè fuga,   729

      190 123   266   27 9   114

25. Ut novi causam mandati,   729

      190 179 205   155

26. Quò jàm raptim eundum,   729

      200 30 240   259

27. Quà tàm diù iter habendum,   729

      161 111 113 174   170

28. Pèr Loca nimirum arida, aspera,   729

      125 54   258   85   207

29. Addè, montuosa, abrupta,   729

      14   401   314

30. Sèd et hæc, inhospita, inaccessa   729

      89 95 16   317   212

31. Nèc non ceca, feralia, squallida, horrida,   729

      38 100 12   102   275   202

32. (Indè diris solùm idonea Feris)   729

      48 172 250   89   170

33. Hiscè, inquam, benè perceptis :   729

      105   220 42   362

34. Heù qualis alme Filj mè adijt angor ;   729

      113 260 36 34 25 113   148

35. Quàm efferæ indè illicò angustiæ :   729

      181 97 48 81   322

36. Quo perdiro dolore affecta :   729

      200 248 169   112

37. Quali in Corde mœrore confecta !   729

      180 39 122 210   178

38. Mihi citò dolor adfuit ineffabilis :
$\overset{46}{}\ \overset{142}{}\ \overset{164}{}\ \ \overset{210}{}\ \ \ \ \overset{167}{}$ 729

39. Summus item mœror.
$\overset{400}{}\ \ \ \ \ \overset{124}{}\ \ \ \overset{205}{}$ 729

40. Vitâ propemodum defeci, concidi,
$\overset{200}{}\ \ \ \ \overset{399}{}\ \ \ \ \ \overset{32}{}\ \ \ \overset{98}{}$ 729

41. Et re vera plenè concidissem,
$\overset{95}{}\ \overset{75}{}\ \overset{176}{}\ \overset{100}{}\ \ \ \ \overset{283}{}$ 729

42. Ac plenè spiritu defecissem,
$\overset{4}{}\ \ \ \overset{100}{}\ \ \ \ \overset{408}{}\ \ \ \ \overset{217}{}$ 729

43. Si à mæstis ijs aversa,
$\overset{89}{}\overset{1}{}\ \ \overset{284}{}\ \ \overset{98}{}\ \ \overset{257}{}$ 729

44. Ad ea alia gaudiosa nate conversa,
$\overset{5}{}\ \ \overset{6}{}\ \ \overset{21}{}\ \ \ \overset{242}{}\ \ \ \overset{126}{}\ \ \ \overset{329}{}$ 729

45. Non altè mœrorem effregissem,
$\overset{100}{}\ \overset{106}{}\ \ \ \overset{230}{}\ \ \ \ \ \overset{293}{}$ 729

46. Nèc ad alta gaudia prosilijssem,
$\overset{38}{}\ \overset{5}{}\ \overset{102}{}\ \ \overset{122}{}\ \ \ \ \ \overset{462}{}$ 729

47. Attamèn ubi illa eadem ego recogito,
$\overset{237}{}\ \ \ \ \overset{111}{}\ \overset{30}{}\ \ \ \overset{35}{}\ \ \ \overset{52}{}\ \ \ \overset{264}{}$ 729

48. Dolor ille plenè resurgit,
$\overset{164}{}\ \overset{34}{}\ \overset{100}{}\ \ \ \overset{431}{}$ 729

49. Dirè redit insimùl mœror,
$\overset{88}{}\ \ \overset{178}{}\ \ \overset{258}{}\ \ \ \overset{205}{}$ 729

50. Et indè ad necem usquè dilanior ;
$\overset{95}{}\ \overset{48}{}\ \overset{5}{}\ \ \overset{63}{}\ \ \ \ \overset{345}{}\ \ \ \overset{173}{}$ 729

51. Ac nè ea recogitem meæ Animæ nulla jùs.
$\overset{4}{}\ \overset{35}{}\ \overset{6}{}\ \ \ \overset{249}{}\ \ \ \ \overset{30}{}\ \ \ \overset{65}{}\ \ \ \overset{151}{}\ \overset{189}{}$ 729

52. Hic mala, nedùm imminent, adsunt ;
$\overset{20}{}\ \ \overset{32}{}\ \ \ \overset{159}{}\ \ \ \ \overset{213}{}\ \ \ \ \overset{305}{}$ 729

53. Ac tàm validè sibi vendicant Cor,
$\overset{4}{}\ \ \overset{111}{}\ \ \overset{129}{}\ \ \overset{100}{}\ \ \ \overset{272}{}\ \ \ \overset{113}{}$ 729

54. Ut nèc animo ab eisdem averti,
$\overset{190}{}\ \overset{38}{}\ \overset{100}{}\ \ \overset{3}{}\ \ \overset{123}{}\ \ \ \overset{275}{}$ 729

55. Nèc sic ad jucunda converti,
   38 92 5   247   347
   729

56. Hodiè aut velim, aut valeam ;
   66   191 144 191 137
   729

57. Soli amodò sum addicta dolori ;
   139 105 200 112 173
   729

58. Ei mihi deindè est tradendum Cor ;
   14 46 57 175 324 113
   729

59. Ac ipsum omni gaudio denegandum.
   4 259 99 161 206
   729

60. Ad hoc ea mala mè cogunt præsentia,
   5 51 6 32 25 270 340
   729

61. Ad hoc et Amor ipse jàm mè adigit, alligat
   5 51 95 131 144 30 25 120 128
   729

62. Et hos dolores cogor amare,
   95 128 249 160 97
   729

63. Id enim mi Fili amabile, quod jubet Amor.
   13 64 29 34 48 204 206 131
   729

JOSEPHUS MAZZA.

MATT. vii. 24.

Ædificavit domum suam supra petram. 322

CAB. 322 SIMPLEX.

Sanctus Corradus Confallonerius.
Anathemata B. Conrado.

This and the cabala of Matt. xxvi. 20 date from a little before 1621, and are the earliest specimens of the Biblical *anagramma numericum* I have met with. They are taken from a collection of anagrams and other literary devices composed in honour of the left arm of the above saint, when it was brought as a relic to his native town of Placentia (Piacenza) in 1620.

Another numerical literary device, called *supputatio*, gives the circumstances and exact date thus :—

De Divi Conradi Brachio
Placentiam translato
Supputatio per numeros minores

(*i.e.*, CAB. SIMPLEX).

Brachium	69	Ab Reverendo	98
Sinistrum	128	Alberto	65
Sancti	60	Degano	42
Conradi	58	Die octava	73
Confalonerii	109	Mensis	71
Anachoritæ	87	Novembris	104
Ex Netina	82	Anno	38
Urbe	42	Salutis	91
Ad Cives	58	Nostræ	82
Placentinos	114		———
Transferetur	149		1620

These *supputationes* soon fell out of fashion, and hardly went beyond the circle of the literary dilettanti round about Piacenza, which included J. B. Spadius, Hieronymus Spadius, and Josephus Folianus, of Modena by birth, but a citizen of Piacenza. H. Spadius edited the collection, and J. Folianus gave a good synopsis of the cabalistic artifices and how they came into vogue.

MATT. xvi. 18.	PER CAB. ORD.
Tu es Petra, et hic super hanc Petram ædificabo Ecclesiam meam.	Franciscus Gottf. Carol. Ioan. Anton. Comes à Ostein. 1743
· 1743	

In the year 1743 there was a vacancy in the Archiepiscopal See of Mentz, and a curious pamphlet was issued, entitled *Vox interrogans*, in which the claims of the Count of Ostein were defended by elaborate anagrammatic proof. The above was the only Scriptural one, and the text was slightly changed to include the year 1743. This and the following example are the only two I have met with on this famous text. One would have expected more.

MATT. xvi. 18.		CABALA SIMPLEX.*	
Tu es Petrus,	148	Joannes	69
et super hanc	118	Marcus	67
Petram	65	Rosettus	123
Ædificabo	53	Petinæ	63
Ecclesiam	64	Ecclesiæ	57
Meam	28	Antistes	97
	476		476

A. CARRARIA, *Triumphus, etc., Milan.*

MATT. xxiv. 7.

Es wird sich empören ein Volck
über das ander, und ein Königreich
über das ander.   4769

PER CAB. TRIG. (4769).
(*"Whigs and Tories"!!*)

Die zwei streitende Factionen in
Engelland Whiggs und Torrys.

J. F. RIEDERER.

MATT. xxiv. 45.		CABALA SIMPLEX.	
Fidelis servus	153	Illustrissimus et	221
Et prudens	110	Reverendissimus	181
Quem constituet	182	D.D. Franciscus	111
Dominus	85	Sanctæ	57
Super	71	Romanæ	59
Familiam suam	106	Ecclesię	57
Ut det illis	119	Presbyter	114
In tempore	103	Cardinalis	82
Tritici	82	Sacratus	92
Mensuram	92	Ferrariensis	129
	1103		1103

J. B. SPADIUS,
De F. Sacrato, S.R.E. Card.

---

* On the occasion of the election of Rosetti to a small bishopric in Italy.

MATT. xxv. 20.

Domine, quinque talenta tradidisti mihi.   355

CAB. 355 SIMPLEX.

Divus Corradus Anachoreta Placentinus.

Anathemata B. Conrado.

MATT. xxvii. 25.		PER CAB. TRIG.	
Da	11	Die	. 70
antwortete	1181	Hebräer	376
das gantze	617	Weyland	690
Volck	442	Gottes	699
und sprache	813	Volck	442
Sein	322	der	178
Blut	469	beschnittene	853
komme	331	verachtete	831
über uns	853	Hauff	289
und über	692	der sämbtlichen	880
unsere	655	Christen .	707
Kinder	369	ärgste Feind	740
	6755		6755

MATT. xxviii. 18.

Data est ei potestas in Cœlo et in terra.   1359

PER CAB. ord.

Causa veræ lętitiæ veri gaudii. 1359

MARC. xii. 11.

Mirabile in oculis nostris.   1045

PER CAB. ord.

En Præsul Magnę Ecclesię Toletanę.   1045

MARC. xii. 11.

Est mirabile in oculis nostris. 1186

CABALA EX Ps. lxxxv. 11.

Veritas de terra orta est.   1186

MARC. xii. 14.

Viam Dei in veritate docens.   999

PER CAB. ord.

Pręsul Magnę Ecclesię Toletanę.
                                999
Naturę miraculum.   999

Luc. i. 13.		Per Cab. Trig.	
Aber der	350	Carolus	712
Engel sprach	702	Sextus	1010
zu ihm	669	Dei	70
Fürchte dich	728	Gratia	418
nicht dann	561	Romanorum	974
dein Gebet	412	Imperator	860
ist erhört	1058	Semper	552
und dein Weib	766	Augustus	1191
Elisabet	506	&	205
wird dir	647	Hispaniarum	951
einen Sohn	660	Rex	421
gebären	306		
	7365		7365

J. F. Riederer.*

Luc. i. 28.	Per Cab. ord.
Ave, Maria, gratiâ plena; Dominus tecum. 1412	Ave Templum Sanctissimæ Triadis. 1412

San Juan.†

* This was fulfilled by the Empress Elizabeth Christina in 1715, and the *Europaische Fama*, No. 177, compliments Riederer on his vaticination and (see Gen. xxviii. 3, 4) quotes another he had made.

† What I am going to remark upon this most excellent specimen of the cabalistic art will, I think, on the first reading of it, appear absolutely incredible and impossible. For *Ave Templum Sanctissimæ Triadis* is certainly such an extremely ingenious and appropriate cabalistic interpretation of the words of the Angel in Luke i. 28, that those readers who have come so far as this in my book, and have realised the difficulties that have to be met in composing a really good and suitable *cabalisticon* on Biblical texts, will no doubt agree that here we have one hard to beat, or even match. Moreover, as it stands alone on the right hand or cabalistical column of this Bible, this would seem an additional reason for supposing it had no fellows or equals, or even inferiors.

What will be thought when I assert that I could easily from my own shelves of rarities produce nine or ten thousand other examples, most of them equally good, and some certainly better, and all accurately counting up the required number of the text in the same true cabalistical way—*i.e., per cabalam ordinariam,* as the example in my

| Ave, Maria, gratia plena. | 651 | Purior angelis. | 651 |
| | | En spes nostra. | 651 |

Maria Deo soli cedit
Hæc enim Dei est jam Imago,
Imago Deo vere simillima,
Plane mira infinita
Et ideo Deo hæc amabilior
Ea ei Pulchrior :
Ac amore hinc ardens
(Oh ! mirabile dictu)

| Ave, gratia plena. | 380 | In, sed ab illâ fit caro, | 380 |

Iam illic ea caro Deus ;
Mater Dei Puella ;
Adde concepit illibata :
Ea non a carnali semine,
A Cœlesti Flamine plena.
Oh rara prodigia !
Oh Dignitas alta !
Oh Gaudia plane Diva !

JOSEPHUS MAZZA.

text. Nay, I could bring nearly five hundred examples in Italian as well ; and this is the only text in the whole Bible to which such remarks are applicable.

The explanation of all this is simple enough when we hear it. These first six words of the Angelical Salutation have always been special favourites with the anagram makers, ever since Joannes Baptista Agnensis, the blind dependent of Cardinal Julius Rospigliosus, sent forth his first hundred in 1661, which were so much admired. Before he died, he made over a thousand, all pure and appropriate ; and more marvellous still, a Pole, in 1702, sent forth a folio containing three thousand anagrams, all in the elegiac metre, and with other men's attempts my shelves contain nearly ten thousand specimens, all different !

Now, although the composition of an anagram is worked out in a way very different from the arithmetical process necessary for a good example of cabalistic art, still, when the anagram is completed, and the full number of letters appropriately used, if we count up the letters by any cabalistical progression we like to use, we get the same numerical result as would be obtained by counting up by the same cabalistical progression previously used the letters of the *programma*, from which the *anagramma* was derived.

Thus in the way of numeration all these anagrams are the *cabalistica* of the

Dominus tecum.   761   Ora pro populo
                                    Insignis Virgo Maria
                                    Cęlum terris unis.   SAN JUAN.

O Benedicta in mulieribus.   913   Templum Hierusalem.
                                    Fons pietatis et lętitię
                                    Mater pietatis et clementiæ,
                                    Illumina me luce tua.

En Benedicta in mulieribus.   908   Tu gloria Jerusalem.

Benedicta in mulieribus.   863   Gaude Mater inviolata
                                    Pura Mater Agni Immolati
                                    Ne derelinquas me in via.

                                                SAN JUAN.

LUC. i. 36, 37.

Und sihe Elisabeth ist auch
schwanger mit einem Sohn und
geht jetzt im sechsten Mond, die
im Geschrey ist, dass Sie un-
fruchtbar sey. Dann bey Gott ist
kein Ding unmöghlich.   11,402

PROGNOSTICON CABALISTICUM.*

Die Allerdurchleuchtigste Fürstin
und Frau, Frau Elizabeth Christina
der regierenden Römischen Kayserlichen Majestät Herrn Herrn
Caroli Sexti unschätzbare Gemahlin.

                              11,402

J. F. RIEDERER.

original *programma*, and consequently in the present instance of Luc. i. 28, they are
cabalistica of that text, although not made with that intention. But not one of the
ten thousand anagrams was made by the arithmetical process which brought forth
Ave Templum Sanctissimæ Triadis, for that is a *cabalisticon* without being an anagram,
and no variation of the letters as they stand could ever make it an anagram. It was
produced by the arithmetical-cabalistic process, and stands *alone* (as far as I know)
against the myriad host which have been evolved out of this one text. I have found
a few on *portions* of the Salutation, as above.

* On the accouchement of the Empress of Charles VI. Appropriately (?) sent to
the Court periodical, *Europaische Fama*, in December, 1715, in the sixth month of
Her Majesty's conception.

Luc. i. 39.

497   101   111   39   212

EXURGENS MARIA ABIJT IN MONTANA   960

     71   27   5   221   169   292   175
1. Ignem Cœli, ad altiora deferri, Natura est :   960

     9   309   20   380   212   30
2. Dè summis hic ortus, fugit ima,   960

     274   30   225   219   100   112
3. Viquè jàm pollens, otiari non amat ;   960

     58   45   81   228   200   348
4. Idèo eò illicò tendit, quò propendit,   960

     95   401   355   109
5. Et quantum potest, facit.   960

     493   9   98   101   20   239
6. Testimonium dè ijs MARIA hic perhibet ;   960

     16   140   70   294   52   170   18   74   30   96
7. Eccè ipsa Cœlico plenissima Igne, quià Dei Filio jàm plena   960*

     39   212   5   210   5   135   42   197   115
8. In Montana, àd Elisabeth, àd Joannem benè celerrimè accedit   960

     35   190   1   109   128   305   192
9. En ut à Gabriele didicit concepisse Cognatam,   960

     4   225   292   9   58   169   39   164
10. Ac, mirante Natura, dè Cœlo fœcundam in senio,   960

     48   93   231   342   246
11. Indè celer pergit, currit, advolat.   960

     4   39   85   42   166   38   114   113   169   190
12. Ac in sè benè conscia, nèc arcani haùd certa consilij   960

     6   30   100   255   4   265   129   171
13. Ea, jàm Deifera, Parenti, ac Puero, Deum fert.   960

     171   116   95   66   49   101   172   190
14. Fert sanè, & hodiè ibidèm facta docent Prodigia   960

     223   32   105   178   100   136   186
15. Tùnc alma MARIÆ verba plenè emula Verbi   960

     69   96   186   266   86   117   140
16. Imò planè Verbi verbis ferè magis admiranda   960

     39   114   40   93   61   190   423
17. In electa almi Filioli Anima prodigia conglobarunt.   960

     51   16   384   296   213
18. Nàm eccè spretis Naturæ legibus,   960

* This line = 959, for Igne = 51.

19.   264   218   158   320

		264 218 158 320	

19. Omnique illius ordine conculcato,   264 218 158 320   960

231 290 291 148
20. Virginea statim operante voce,   960

224 225 1 49 27 105 150 179
21. Nondùm Puer à Deo Cœli fit mente Vir.   960

69 292 34 163 48 354
22. Imò talibus ille donis indè impletur,   960

212 118 96 534
23. Tanta luce planè perfunditur,   960

186 1 179 236 220 138
24. Tales à Triade recipit Amoris flammas,   960

190 20 129 132 39 186 264
25. Ut ibi Deum Hominem in Matre dignoscat ;   960

20 299 191 95 145 210
26. Ibi cognitum humillimè, et acclinis adoret,   960

95 326 50 162 122 205
27. Et adoratum adeò accenso corde rediligat   960

190 120 20 355 275
28. Ut valdè ibi concitus æstu,   960

95 20 321 85 356 39 44
29. Et ibi subitò sè vertat in faciem,   960

95 57 308 500
30. Et deindè lætissimè exultet   960

4 20 81 125 108 161 361 100
31. Ac ibi illicò prę nimio gaudio saltus edat.   960

35 16 100 317 314 178
32. En hæc omnia ediderunt Virginis verba.   960

89 35 21 210 605
33. Sèd en alia præclara supersunt :   960

5 26 105 168 48 406 202
34. Ad eam MARIÆ vocem indè exulat Satan :   960

247 96 453 164
35. Paterna planè profligatur culpa,   960

48 169 496 65 182
36. Indè immensæ profluunt Animæ Gratiæ,   960

95 173 66 220 186 4 216
37. Et certè hodiè tòt, tales, ac tantæ,   960

190 95 274 401
38. Ut et Paraclito repleatur,   960

39. $\overset{314}{\text{Illumquè}}$ $\overset{150}{\text{tandèm}}$ $\overset{190}{\text{Matri}}$ $\overset{306}{\text{refundat,}}$ 960

40. $\overset{159}{\text{Nulli}}$ $\overset{230}{\text{subindè}}$ $\overset{175}{\text{nævo}}$ $\overset{34}{\text{ille}}$ $\overset{85}{\text{sè}}$ $\overset{277}{\text{subdat,}}$ 960

41. $\overset{380}{\text{Agiocosmus}}$ $\overset{266}{\text{posteà}}$ $\overset{208}{\text{certò}}$ $\overset{106}{\text{fiat}}$ 960

42. $\overset{496}{\text{Tantusvè}}$ $\overset{34}{\text{ille}}$ $\overset{277}{\text{habeatur}}$ $\overset{39}{\text{in}}$ $\overset{114}{\text{Juda,}}$ 960

43. $\overset{190}{\text{Ut}}$ $\overset{42}{\text{benè}}$ $\overset{110}{\text{firmè}}$ $\overset{343}{\text{credatur}}$ $\overset{275}{\text{Mæssias,}}$ 960

44. $\overset{4}{\text{Ac}}$ $\overset{76}{\text{Plebi,}}$ $\overset{140}{\text{major}}$ $\overset{281}{\text{omnibus}}$ $\overset{277}{\text{dicatur}}$ $\overset{3}{\text{ab}}$ $\overset{179}{\text{Ipso.}}$ 960

45. $\overset{48}{\text{Oh}}$ $\overset{122}{\text{ergò}}$ $\overset{105}{\text{MARIÆ}}$ $\overset{340}{\text{Vox}}$ $\overset{30}{\text{jàm}}$ $\overset{180}{\text{verè}}$ $\overset{135}{\text{miranda!}}$ 960

46. $\overset{48}{\text{Oh}}$ $\overset{449}{\text{Virtus,}}$ $\overset{49}{\text{Deo}}$ $\overset{198}{\text{Numini}}$ $\overset{42}{\text{benè}}$ $\overset{174}{\text{finitima!}}$ 960

47. $\overset{48}{\text{Oh}}$ $\overset{262}{\text{Charitas}}$ $\overset{39}{\text{in}}$ $\overset{101}{\text{MARIA}}$ $\overset{104}{\text{mirè}}$ $\overset{406}{\text{properosa!}}$ 960

48. $\overset{89}{\text{Sèd}}$ $\overset{95}{\text{et}}$ $\overset{344}{\text{insupèr}}$ $\overset{42}{\text{benè}}$ $\overset{104}{\text{mirè}}$ $\overset{286}{\text{Operosa!}}$ 960

49. $\overset{48}{\text{Oh}}$ $\overset{30}{\text{jàm}}$ $\overset{230}{\text{concepti}}$ $\overset{280}{\text{Emmanuelis}}$ $\overset{186}{\text{Mater}}$ $\overset{30}{\text{jàm}}$ $\overset{156}{\text{Homogenea!}}$ 960

50. $\overset{49}{\text{Deo,}}$ $\overset{4}{\text{ac}}$ $\overset{27}{\text{Cœli}}$ $\overset{178}{\text{Gratia}}$ $\overset{96}{\text{plena,}}$ $\overset{42}{\text{hanc,}}$ $\overset{95}{\text{et}}$ $\overset{149}{\text{illum}}$ $\overset{142}{\text{citò}}$ $\overset{178}{\text{affert}}$ 960

51. $\overset{190}{\text{Ut}}$ $\overset{66}{\text{hodiè}}$ $\overset{119}{\text{Joanni,}}$ $\overset{210}{\text{Elisabeth,}}$ $\overset{184}{\text{adsit}}$ $\overset{191}{\text{Emmanuel,}}$ 960

52. $\overset{38}{\text{Nèc}}$ $\overset{146}{\text{tamèn}}$ $\overset{184}{\text{adsit}}$ $\overset{128}{\text{nisi,}}$ $\overset{190}{\text{ut}}$ $\overset{274}{\text{Jesus,}}$ 960

53. $\overset{188}{\text{Idest}}$ $\overset{470}{\text{persolvens,}}$ $\overset{302}{\text{salvans;}}$ 960

54. $\overset{14}{\text{Adde,}}$ $\overset{281}{\text{omnibus}}$ $\overset{251}{\text{ornans,}}$ $\overset{214}{\text{ditans,}}$ $\overset{4}{\text{àc}}$ $\overset{196}{\text{Magnificans.}}$ 960

55. $\overset{124}{\text{Dùm}}$ $\overset{122}{\text{ergò}}$ $\overset{111}{\text{talia}}$ $\overset{20}{\text{ibi}}$ $\overset{239}{\text{sedulò}}$ $\overset{118}{\text{efficis}}$ $\overset{226}{\text{Virgo,}}$ 960

56. $\overset{257}{\text{Ecquis}}$ $\overset{100}{\text{non}}$ $\overset{90}{\text{magnificè}}$ $\overset{95}{\text{Te}}$ $\overset{106}{\text{Magnificam}}$ $\overset{125}{\text{canat,}}$ $\overset{4}{\text{ac}}$ $\overset{183}{\text{efferat?}}$ 960

57. $\overset{115}{\text{Vel}}$ $\overset{230}{\text{tuo}}$ $\overset{69}{\text{illo}}$ $\overset{176}{\text{Cantico}}$ $\overset{100}{\text{non}}$ $\overset{42}{\text{benè}}$ $\overset{228}{\text{decantet?}}$ 960

58. $\overset{51}{\text{Nàm}}$ $\overset{39}{\text{in}}$ $\overset{95}{\text{Tè}}$ $\overset{101}{\text{MARIA}}$ $\overset{110}{\text{Tibi}}$ $\overset{251}{\text{maxima}}$ $\overset{189}{\text{Deus}}$ $\overset{124}{\text{effecit,}}$ 960

91 39 109 100   100   75   100 128   218
59. At in alijs plenè omnia dona non nisi Tecùm :   960
101 85 64   443   38 96   133
60. Facta es enim adjutorium illi planè simile ;   960
199 95 10 60   596
61. Quin et Adæ pia Conredemptrix ;   960
223   190 40 104   86   4   90   223
62. Ideòque Tù ò Domina, Magnifica, ac magnificè Dominum   960
105   131 123 71   143   176   61 26   124
63. Amodò unà cū almo Domino, Magnificat anima mea Dominā. 960

JOSEPHUS MAZZA.

Luc. i. 42.	Per Cab. ord.
Benedictus fructus ventris tui. 1970	Cunctorum gloria decusque mortalium. 1970

Luc. i. 48.	Per Cab. ord.
Respexit Deus humilitatem Ancillę suę. 1853	Quasi mirrha electa dedit suavitatem odoris. 1853

Luc. i. 48.	Per Cab. ord.
Beatam te dicunt omnes generationes. 1245	Salve Lactatrix Christi. 1245 Virginem adora e spina macula tutam. 1245 O Remedium totius mundi. 1245

Luc. i. 49.	Per Cab. ord.
Fecit magna qui potens est. 1021	Originariæ maculæ munda est. 1021 Munda puritatis imago. 1021

SAN JUAN.

Luc. i. 59.
SOLILOQUIUM.

430   301   345
VENERUNT CIRCUMCIDERE PUERUM   1076
34 16 161 98 20 30   414 3 300
1. Filj eccè nobis Dies Hic, jàm octavus ab Ortu ;   1076

6

      280   342   158   296

2. Estvè secundum ordine Sabbatum ;   1076

     304   237   13 180   342

3. Neutri attamèn, id verè secundum ;   1076

   199   111   332   434

4. Quìn tàm nefastum utriquè,   1076

  190 105 179 150   384   5   63

5. Ut amodò sit Nos acturum ad necem,   1076

  95 100   270   154   136   5   316

6. Te, ità tenellum, indebitè addicens ad Vulnera.   1076

  190   218   253   71   97   247

7. Mèquè Tècum doloris gladio amarè confodiens.   1076

  113   164   20   161 115 140 73 235   55

8. Heù dolor ! Hic Nobis vel ipsa bona fiunt malefica.   1076

  35 115   343   405   146   32

9. En vel fœlicitatum Numerus indicat mala,   1076

  95 39 140   280   226   296

10. Et in ipsa cubatione designat acerbitatem,   1076

  89 95 203   213   106 160 210

11. Sèd et afferens nefasta altè, prò gaudijs,   1076

  99   175   214   249 66 108   165

12. Omni eliminata lætitia, dolores hodiè addit immanes ; 1076

  165   220   215   66   245   165

13. Immanes inquam, adeòquè hodiè ambobus immanes, 1076

  190 303   295   135 26 127

14. Ut horrore depressa, Mens mea deficiat,   1076

  95 113 115 1 170 266 86   230

15. Et Cor, vel à solo pavore, ferè depereat.   1076

  110 216 113 260 30   183   164

16. Tibi autèm heù qualis jàm imminet dolor !   1076

  35 34 159 89 79 469   211

17. En Filj, sacer, sèd acer arripitur Gladius,   1076

  95 133 528   320

18. Tè læthali secturus vulnere,   1076

  95 250 10 88   246   137   250

19. Et quasi Adæ dirè deperditi germen esses,   1076

  4 108   381   239   344

20. Ac ceù Circumcisione indigus expiari,   1076

  45 39 300   109 222 361

21. Eo in tenerrima Carne ictum excipies ;   1076

95   50   48   260   81   39 95 164   244
22. Et hinc, oh qualis illicò in Te dolor adveniet !   1076

  5   280 190   214   387
23. Ad quos Tù cogêris vagitus ?   1076

  241   92   250   493
24. Quas longè evomes lachrymas ?   1076

  4   401   372   299
25. Ac quantum Cruoris emittes ?   1076

  165   320   229   362
26. Quæ præsens meismet auribus,   1076

  279   220   242   100   235
27. Meisquè hicernet oculis plenè sentiam ;   1076

  235   39 125 169   154   354
28. Sentiam, ni præ dolore reddar exanimis,   1076

  246   172   95   282   281
29. Animamquè effundam, Tè Sanguinem effundente.   1076

  91 113   188   205   261   97   121
30. At heù nimium Miseram, planèquè infœlicem Mariam !   1076

  113   169   337   175 282
31. Heù ! immanis inflictus est ictus !   1076

  151   125   156   71   30   254 175 114
32. Tenella etiàm Siliceo Gladio jàm resecta est Caro,   1076

  50   332   137 48 226 283
33. Hinc Divinus itidèm indè effluit Cruor :   1076

  86   336 3 242   409
34. Acerbæ fluunt ab oculis lacrymæ,   1076

  95 169 50 400   362
35. Et dolens adeò anxiaris, convelleris,   1076

  190 6 69   169   180   81   278   103
36. Ut ea plaga, dolore cogente, Animam videaris efflare.   1076

  95 52 180 100 228 5 63 118 95 140
37. Et ego ista omnia videns, ad necem agor, et Ipsa ;   1076

  334   104 39 95 293   211
38. Quiquè modò in Tè sævijt Gladius   1076

  16   34 46 295   81   604
39. Eccè ille meam paritèr Animam pertransivit.   1076

  238 83 4 179 109 400   63
40. Horum acri, ac acerrima vi moreremur Ambo,   1076

  89 30 38 198 118 302   301
41. Si jàm nèc Cœleste illis obesset consilium,   1076

89 38   124   163   271   391
42. Si nèc aliud Mundi Salus exigeret,   1076
89 38 95 141   1   161   366 .   185
43. Si nèc et majora à Nobis appeteret Numen.   1076
59   300   16 89 180   284   148
44. Magna sunt hæc, sèd verè dolorum initia ;   1076
150 64   141   199 95   251   176
45. Nos enìm majora, quìn et maxima manent,   1076
5 165 89 95 25   216 5 107   369
46. Ad quæ, si Tè, Mè, Pater è Cœlis præordinat,   1076
150   217   18   381   310
47. Nos Decreto Dei obsistere, execrabile,   1076
282   161 115   204   314
48. Sicùt Nobis vel effugere impossibile.   1076
15 122   380   248   6   32   161   112
49. Ejà ergò fortitèr obeamus ea Mala Nobis addicta   1076
51   169 180   312   189 175
50. Nàm qui ista disponit, Deus.est :   1076
169 140   244   175 132   216
51. Qui ipsa ordinat, est amans Pater ;   1076
180 122 100 128   210   130   206
52. Verè ergò non nisi optima eligit, jubet :   1076
30   300   192   125 95 5   138   191
53. Jàm vult Homines pèr Tè ad Cœlum reduci   1076
138   25   110 51   260   39   170   283
54. Nècnon, Mè Tibi hoc summo in opere copulari   1076
150   203   95   174 100   354
55. Vellem equidèm Tè pœnis non pervium,   1076
69 52 5   166   95   221   160 95   213
56. Imò ego ad pœnas, Tè incolumi, prò Tè suffici.   1076
340   110 1 49   258   52   266
57. Omnesquè Tibi à Deo decretas ego subire ;   1076
89   108   100 125   215   .132   307
58. Sèd Homo non pèr merum Hominem reparabilis :   1076
190 116 190   132   189   163   96
59. Tù sanè, ut Hominem redimas, perimi debes ;   1076
173   64   124 191   299   225
60. Certè enìm, sinè tua cruenta morte,   1076
38   26   42   424   38 144   10   354
61. Nèc Adam benè redemptus, nèc Ipse Adæ Redemptor,   1076

170 271 100 128 125   282
62. Quià Salus non nisi pèr Sanguinem,   1076

38 164   274   128 95 109   268
63. Nèc eris JESUS, nisi et Carne cæsus.   1076

JOSEPHUS MAZZA.

Luc. ii. 7.

Soliloquium.

327   125   39   309
RECLINAVIT EUM IN PRÆSEPIO   800

139   278   126   194 29 34
1. Siccinè nasceris Dilecte Jesu mi Filj?   800

95   126   4   52   110 200   213
2. Et frigidam, ac algidam tibi Seligis Brumam,   800

100 128   403   96   39   34
3. Non nisi Stabulum habes in Ædem,   800

69 160 48   134   389
4. Imò prò blanda Cuna Præsepium,   800

95 296 51   65 160 133
5. Et stramen hoc fœnile prò cubili   800

209   159   218   214
6. Inops etenim Inopis Filius   800

200 200 42 262   96
7. Nequè quo benè tegaris, habes ;   800

89 20 95 50   314 39 193
8. Sèd hic et glaciali nudus in Bruma,   800

16 51 183   456   94
9. Eccè hoc rudi obvolueris lineo :   800

35 111 238   301   115
10. En tàm despecta reciperis Caula,   800

190 187 300 1 122
11. Ut gravi tremens à Gelu   800

200   200   311   38 51
12. Nequè Pannis fovearis, nèc Igne.   800

96 95 128   481
13. Planè Tè algor excruciat,   800

95 295 59   161 190
14. Tè paritèr hoccè fœnum offendit.   800

$$100 \quad 230 \quad 470$$
15. Ità subindè tortus   800

$$225 \quad 201 \quad 205 \quad 169$$
16. Summè rigens, plenèvè dolens,   800

$$106 \quad 324 \quad 201 \quad 169$$
17. Altè agentibus, rigore, dolore   800

$$48 \quad 320 \quad 94 \quad 9 \quad 231 \quad 98$$
18. Oh ! tremorem adis ; ah ? fletum edis,   800

$$38 \quad 121 \quad 3 \quad 160 \quad 20 \quad 64 \quad 215 \quad 179$$
19. Nèc ulla ab ullo hic piæ Spes opis.   800

$$89 \quad 138 \quad 66 \quad 319 \quad 188$$
20. Si Cœlum hodiè precibus advoco,   800

$$276 \quad 14 \quad 160 \quad 5 \quad 115 \quad 230$$
21. Ferreum, adde, Æneum, ad opem reperiam,   800

$$4 \quad 221 \quad 113 \quad 36 \quad 426$$
22. Ac orans haùd fiam exorans.   800

$$89 \quad 192 \quad 31 \quad 151 \quad 116 \quad 221$$
23. Si Homines adeam, barbarè sanè repellar.   800

$$323 \quad 30 \quad 132 \quad 5 \quad 310$$
24. Venisti jàm amans ad tuos,   800

$$91 \quad 97 \quad 95 \quad 300 \quad 217$$
25. At Impij Tè nolunt recipere ;   800

$$50 \quad 3 \quad 94 \quad 653$$
26. Hinc ab eis reyectus,   800

$$30 \quad 266 \quad 96 \quad 5 \quad 403$$
27. Jàm confugere debes àd Stabulum.   800

$$97 \quad 275 \quad 428$$
28. His Bestijs associandus ;   800

$$48 \quad 137 \quad 125 \quad 490$$
29. Oh fallor ; etiàm posthabendus :   800

$$182 \quad 34 \quad 228 \quad 356$$
30. Habeberis Filj ipsis despectior ;   800

$$223 \quad 20 \quad 159 \quad 290 \quad 108$$
31. Ideòquè hic, nèdum quanti Homo,   800

$$89 \quad 30 \quad 38 \quad 125 \quad 290 \quad 128 \quad 100$$
32. Sèd jàm nèc etiàm, quanti Bellua, fies.   800

$$35 \quad 122 \quad 20 \quad 508 \quad 3 \quad 112$$
33. En ergò hic contemptus ab Homine.   800

$$9 \quad 137 \quad 351 \quad 303$$
34. Ah ! Itidèm Brutis miserior,   800

168 316 1 315
35. Omnimodè ignoraris à cunctis,   800

396 124 1 279
36. Aspernaris itèm à Tuis.   800

48 264 113 140 235
37. Oh pudor ! heù deflebilis pietas !   800

89 99 79 227 306
38. Si ! Dicebare olìm Hominum Desiderium, 800

89 272 180 95 164
39. Sèd posthac diceris, et eris   800

173 242 95 290
40. Odium, Abominatio, et peripsema.   800

100 289 115 156 140
41. Non rependent, vel Amorem amori,   800

69 126 160 391 54
42. Imò jugia prò dilectionibus odia,   800

160 269 161 32 93 4 81
43. Prò ineffabilibus Bonis mala effera, ac infanda. 800

200 39 96 465
44. Quò in amando profusior,   800

45 173 292 290
45. Eò certè odiosior habitus,   800

95 48 356 139 162
46. Et indè despectior, undè amabilior.   800

38 151 38 98 104 34 337
47. Nèc insana, nèc falsa modo Filj prænuncio : 800

16 64 180 276 95 169
48. Ecce enim verè Pauper, et Dolens.   800

3 406 20 190 181
49. Ab Angustijs hic incipis Annos.   800

184 107 309 200
50. Compar decet ortui Vita ;   800

50 199 246 92 213
51. Hinc uti cœpisti, sic desines.   800

95 52 105 39 174 77 34 95 129
52. Et ego hisce in pœnis bone Filj te cernam ? 800

38 225 80 122 38 48 51 38 160
53. Nèc summè doleam Corde, nèc indè defleam, nèc depeream ? 800

111 96 206 131 38 218
54. Hùc planè ducit amor, nèc sinit.   800

^{51   149   304   107   189}
55. Nàm læthalem profecto ciet dolorem,   800

^{89   46   144   274   105   142}
56. Sèd mihi emori prohibet, deflere denegat ;   800

^{300   230   190   80}
57. Vult vivam, ut doleam.   800

^{89   118   251   95   131   116}
58. Sèd vide quònam tè Amor adegit,   800

^{110   88   190   198   95   119}
59. Nempè, dirè ut angaris, et angas :   800

^{218   146   47   116   100   173}
60. Tecùm tamen angi sanè non abnuo.   800

^{91   13   99   204   213   100   80}
61. At id doleo quod coæquè non doleam,   800

^{170   169   100   149   100   112}
62. Quià qui non dolet, non amat,   800

^{320   66   89   100   225}
63. Propèvè nihil, si non summè.   800

Josephus Mazza.

Luc. ii. 35.

Soliloquium.

^{211   328   81   506   211}
TUAM IPSIUS ANIMAM PERTRANSIBIT GLADIUS   1337

^{40 194 40 34   206   34   156   253   380}
1. O Jesu, ò Filj ; Cordis mei Fons doloris æternus !   1337

^{36   34   169   25   123   4   125   253   71   197   300}
2. Alme Filj, qui mè diro, ac jugi doloris Gladio cernis côfossam,   1337

^{95   20   124   249   181   355   313}
3. Et hic sinè requie aliqua doloribus cumulari :   1337

^{173   175   204   184   16   93   242   27   223}
4. Quid est quod Simeon hæc effera adjungat Cœli præsagia,   1337

^{313   123   150   9   367   161   191   23}
5. Vocequè fatidica Nos dè futura nobis, admoneat clade ?   1337

^{95   39   246   508   240   159   1   49}
6. Tè, in signum contradictionis, Terræ dandum à Deo,   1337

^{388   223   25   355   97   249}
7. Acutisvè affirmans, mè doloribus efferè sauciandam ?   1337

8. 31 100 92 102 420 496 58 38
    Àn non longè acerbam tuorum cruciatuum Iliadem didici,   1337

9. 138 65 182 164 263 117 408
    Nècnon meo sub memori Pectore condo, percurro?   1337

10. 31 100 205 194 165 99 204 339
    Àn non ex ejus memoria, omni impleor amaritudine;   1337

11. 218 140 410 253 316
    Corvè admiranda patitur doloris vulnera?   1337

12. 216 98 285 20 242 124 12 55 285
    Quænam dies quæsò hic deperijt, sinè hac linea dolorosa?   1337

13. 235 115 195 211 379 50 152
    Quandò vel tuæ peracerbæ Passionis adeò oblita,   1337

14. 115 184 83 95 50 180 410 220
    Vel veri ergà Tè adeò verè expers amoris,   1337

15. 190 38 150 110 258 425 166
    Ùt nèc mente, Tibi decretas, revolverem pœnas,   1337

16. 38 34 39 420 102 200 294 210
    Nèc illæ eædem revolutæ amplam darent mœroris messem?   1337

17. 29 36 34 89 144 89 231 304 242 139
    Mi Alme Filj, si pedes, si manus fixis oculis videam,   1337

18. 180 81 234 394 448
    Verè illicò clavos excogito terebrantes: 1337

19. 89 281 305 30 385 197 50
    Si latus intuear, jàm occurrit celerrimè Lancea,   1337

20. 185 39 440 26 264 383
    Ibiquè in Mortuum eam recogito insævientem;   1337

21. 38 311 5 148 125 58 142 244 266
    Nèc unquam àd, ipsi etiàm Cœlo, adorabile caput respicio, · 1337

22. 199 81 143 321 250 100 243
    Quin illicò Alapas, sputa, spinas plenè commemorem.   1337

23. 89 314 358 39 122 50 365
    Si Dorsum contemplor, in Corde Flagella revolvo: 1337

24. 97 39 229 391 189 9 383
    His in Ulnis excipiens, cogito dè apprehensione: 1337

25. 164 95 188 154 121 221 394
    Cingens Tè Fascijs, Menti, Lora, Funes obycio.   1337

26. 124 110 255 108 319 140 281
    Dùm defles, Gethsemani Agoniam, sudorem, Ipsa considero. 1337

27. 95 353 228 39 181 120 124 197
    Et Morientis voces, in Cruce dandas, dùm vagis.   1337

125   124   14   481   21 95 219   258

28. Etiàm dùm Lac exsugis, Fel, et Acetum commemoro ;   1337

140 26   100   234   118   273   46   400

29. Ipsa mea omnia oscula, Judæ osculo, mihi amarescunt.   1337

144   398   46   104   444   201

30. Ipse Lectulus mihi diram obycit Crucem.   1337

190   376   191   134   446

31. Ut pauperrima tua Cuna, Sepulchrum,   1337

50   200 89 89   573   336

32. Illam pannis si cingo, syndonis reminiscor.   1337

39 230 210   211   245   210   192

33. In tuo Somno tuam Mortem mœrens aspicio ;   1337

115   231   389   162   440

34. Vel aspiciendo sopitum, lugeo Mortuum :   1337

173 231 173 237 49   245   229

35. Cùr plura, cùr singula Deo sigillatìm depromo ?   1337

30   100 279 169   217 300 242

36. Jàm omnia tuis omninò aperta sunt oculis,   1337

48   170 46 279 197 116   481

37. Indè mentem meam tuis cernis plenam Passionibus,   1337

520   138 113 290   276

38. Doloribusquè idcircò Cor jugitèr occupari.   1337

286   46   211 30 179 504   81

39. Quocircà meam Gladius jàm durè pertransijt Animam,   1337

96 65 39 122 30 113   277 175 420

40. Planè meo in Corde jàm diù inflictum est vulnus.   1337

420 . 285 39 170 320   103

41. Vulnus igitùr in solo vulnere cadet,   1337

51 38 200 39 25 210 38   324   233   179

42. Nàm nèc alius in mè novo illi vulneri, locus aderit.   1337

173 100 300 265 51   264   184

43. Quid sibi vult itaquè hoc Oraculo Simeon ?   1337

278 46 6   333   148   138   388

44. Quidvè mihi ea prophetali Voce Cœlum prænunciat ?   1337

95 59   198   113   360 39 85 388

45. Et magna quidèm Cor anxium in sè obversat.   1337

163 30 32 39 170   219   121   126   92   239   106

46. Nùnc illa mala in esse cognito fore Cordi longè minus penalia 1337

395   159   340 20   423

47. Fortius etenìm præsentia ibi desæviunt.   1337

104   214 35 253   140 110 18 131   233   99

48. Modò timet, nè doloris semen, nēpè Dei Amor, interìm abeat, 1337

  210 100   277   125 164 96   179   186

49. Eòquè ità deperdito, etiàm dolor plane omnis abscedat,   1337

  58 39 191 295   294   460

50. Ideo in tua Passione, iterum renovandus.   1337

  163   149 13 165   311 65   298   173

51. Nùnc demùm id pavida tribuo meo imperfecto Dolori,   1337

  169 211 196 4 116   435   100 106

52. Qui fortè veram, ac plenam summitatem non habet,   1337

  95   202   166   223 46   400   205

53. Et gradatìm incædens, tùnc mihi summus evàdet.   1337

89 13 107 39   269   296   150 24 178 39   133

54. Si id cadit in primum! Naturæ, temne, dele ordinē in dolendo. 1337

  38 100   344   233   105   386   131

55. Nèc non præsentiæ defectum amodò suppleat Amor.   1337

  30 449 140   456   175   87

56. Illa Virtus Amori nullatenùs est deneganda ;   1337

  95 204 34 39 113 145 100 371   116   120

57. Et quod ille in Cor meum non exerat, dedecet valdè.   1337

  342   159 100   253   90   393

58. Secundum, nedùm non approbo, penè execror   1337

  173 216   46 189 1 49   300   363

59. Quid namquè mihi miseræ à Deo contingat deterius,   1337

  181 190 268 1 169 18 20 230 124 136

60. Quàm ut immunis à Dolore, Dei hic vivam sine Amore ?   1337

  48   384   163   369   373

61. Indè tertium censeo potiùs admittendum.   1337

  91 190 169 211   265 1 25   230   155

62. At Tù, qui moras potes à mè tollere, tolle ;   1337

  4 148 40 126   166   251   139   332   131

63. Ac mecũ, ò Dilecte, tarda ignoret molimina Divinus Amor.   1337

JOSEPHUS MAZZA.

Luc. ii. 48.

SOLILOQUIUM.

  34   173   202   161   92

FILJ QUID FECISTI NOBIS SIC ?   662

  200 66   241   126 29

1. Quò hodiè declinasti Dilecte mi,   662

2. $\overset{200}{\text{Tevè}}$ $\overset{111}{\text{ubi}}$ $\overset{30}{\text{jàm}}$ $\overset{321}{\text{recepisti,}}$ 662

3. $\overset{173}{\text{Cùr}}$ $\overset{236}{\text{Patrem}}$ $\overset{253}{\text{deseris}}$?   662

4. $\overset{81}{\text{Infelici}}$ $\overset{46}{\text{mihi}}$ $\overset{95}{\text{Tè}}$ $\overset{440}{\text{subtrahis}}$;   662

5. $\overset{139}{\text{Miro}}$ $\overset{63}{\text{ambo}}$ $\overset{210}{\text{mœrore}}$ $\overset{250}{\text{replens}}$?   662

6. $\overset{89}{\text{Sèd}}$ $\overset{25}{\text{mè}}$ $\overset{173}{\text{certè}}$ $\overset{115}{\text{vèl}}$ $\overset{260}{\text{summo}}$?   662

7. $\overset{9}{\text{Ah}}$ $\overset{126}{\text{Nate,}}$ $\overset{95}{\text{Tè}}$ $\overset{230}{\text{amisso,}}$ $\overset{173}{\text{quid}}$ $\overset{29}{\text{agam}}$?   662

8. $\overset{95}{\text{Tè}}$ $\overset{1}{\text{à}}$ $\overset{25}{\text{mè}}$ $\overset{30}{\text{jàm}}$ $\overset{223}{\text{elongato,}}$ $\overset{173}{\text{quid}}$ $\overset{115}{\text{ero}}$?   662

9. $\overset{248}{\text{Absquè}}$ $\overset{194}{\text{Numine}}$ $\overset{163}{\text{nùnc}}$ $\overset{57}{\text{deficiam}}$;   662

10. $\overset{4}{\text{Ac}}$ $\overset{124}{\text{sinè}}$ $\overset{189}{\text{primo}}$ $\overset{130}{\text{Ente}}$ $\overset{100}{\text{non}}$ $\overset{115}{\text{ero,}}$ 662

11. $\overset{89}{\text{Sèd}}$ $\overset{39}{\text{in}}$ $\overset{186}{\text{nihilum}}$ $\overset{46}{\text{decidam,}}$ $\overset{57}{\text{deindè}}$ $\overset{245}{\text{evanescam.}}$ 662

12. $\overset{91}{\text{At}}$ $\overset{181}{\text{quam}}$ $\overset{132}{\text{vana}}$ $\overset{258}{\text{commemoro}}$!   662

13. $\overset{250}{\text{Utinàm}}$ $\overset{177}{\text{annihilari}}$ $\overset{25}{\text{mè}}$ $\overset{210}{\text{velles}}$!   662

14. $\overset{190}{\text{Mèquè}}$ $\overset{65}{\text{meo}}$ $\overset{106}{\text{nihilo}}$ $\overset{30}{\text{jàm}}$ $\overset{92}{\text{reddi}}$ $\overset{179}{\text{denuò}}$!   662

15. $\overset{109}{\text{Efficiar}}$ $\overset{66}{\text{nihil}}$ $\overset{101}{\text{facta,}}$ $\overset{110}{\text{Tibi}}$ $\overset{113}{\text{haùd}}$ $\overset{163}{\text{odibilis,}}$ 662

16. $\overset{38}{\text{Nèc}}$ $\overset{190}{\text{Tù}}$ $\overset{3}{\text{ab}}$ $\overset{224}{\text{immerita}}$ $\overset{207}{\text{fugies,}}$ 662

17. $\overset{38}{\text{Nèc}}$ $\overset{52}{\text{ego}}$ $\overset{64}{\text{damni}}$ $\overset{86}{\text{pœna}}$ $\overset{48}{\text{indè}}$ $\overset{109}{\text{angar}}$ $\overset{116}{\text{adhùc}}$ $\overset{39}{\text{in}}$ $\overset{110}{\text{Via}}$:   662

18. $\overset{55}{\text{Fio}}$ $\overset{326}{\text{reprobis}}$ $\overset{90}{\text{penè}}$ $\overset{191}{\text{infelicior,}}$ 662

19. $\overset{123}{\text{Cum,}}$ $\overset{34}{\text{Filj,}}$ $\overset{115}{\text{vel}}$ $\overset{214}{\text{vivæ}}$ $\overset{132}{\text{denegas}}$ $\overset{44}{\text{Faciem}}$:   662

20. $\overset{135}{\text{Nonnè}}$ $\overset{16}{\text{hæc,}}$ $\overset{126}{\text{Nate,}}$ $\overset{140}{\text{major}}$ $\overset{159}{\text{Inferni}}$ $\overset{86}{\text{pœna}}$?   662

21. $\overset{89}{\text{Sèd}}$ $\overset{89}{\text{si}}$ $\overset{5}{\text{ad}}$ $\overset{195}{\text{desiderij}}$ $\overset{202}{\text{gradum}}$ $\overset{82}{\text{acerba,}}$ 662

33 151 20 173 65 220		
22. Hèm nulla ibi dolori meo comparanda ;	662
42 20 3 266 245 86		
23. Benè ibi ab inclinatione invalet pœna :	662
39 25 88 284 95 131		
24. In mè dirè sævit et Amor :	662
89 131 113 160 169		
25. Sèd Amor haùd ullò minor,	662
229 334 99		
26. Itemvè flagrantior omni,	662
4 125 169 364		
27. Ac etiàm Cœlicolis comparatis,	662
51 140 281 190		
28. Nàm major omnibus collectim.	662
110 122 104 190 136		
29. Tali ergò modò ardens amore,	662
212 95 50 95 210		
30. Tanta et hinc acta cupidine,	662
113 34 89 24 100 216 86		
31. Amata, Filj, si facie caream, quænam pœna?	662
135 57 219 251		
32. Nonnè deindè omnium maxima?	662
15 116 146 294 91		
33. Ejà Sanè parem nequit habere.	662
95 25 206 106 120 110		
34. Et mè Matrem altè huic addicis?	662
263 110 245 44		
35. Dulcifluam nempè occulis faciem,	662
95 39 110 5 64 106 104 139		
36. Et in via ad damni pœnam mirè cogis.	662
89 106 42 136 289		
37. Sèd pœnam hanc libens amplector,	662
89 100 205 234 34		
38. Si non ex meritò, Filj ;	662
39 25 146 104 164 184		
39. In mè tamèn modò timeo culpam ;	662
284 144 100 134		
40. Justè Ipse omnia faciens	662
250 160 39 18 195		
41. Solùm ardes in labe reos ;	662

                332   228   102
42.   Innocuos nonnisi amas,   662
        123 98 170 110   116   45
43.   Cùm ijs esse, Tibi adhùc deliciæ ;   662
        89 1   480   92
44.   Sèd à deserentibus abis :   662
              163   122   124   253
45.   Nùnc ergò dùm deseris,   662
        124 95 1 25   215   202
46.   Dùm et à mè aufuga fugis :   662
        150   284   228
47.   Nùm culposa videor,   662
            275   30   163   194
48.   Tibiquè jàm odibilis, JESU ?   662
        66   46   122   186   242
49.   Nihil mihi corde consciam noscis,   662
        33   146 39 51   113   280
50.   Hèm tamèn in hoc haùd justa ;   662
          122   249 26   265
51.   Delicta quis mea intelliget ?   662
        190 104   100   268
52.   Tù mirè omnia noscens.   662
        91 262   49   79   181
53.   At siquid Deo odibile gessi,   662
        34 5 95   165   4   165   194
54.   Filj àd Tè veniam, àc veniam poscam,   662
        190   57   42   88   95   190
55.   Tù deindè benè redde Tè Matri,   662
          262   206   52   142
56.   Infelicemquè Matrem blandè recipe ;   662
        254   44   51   6   192   115
57.   Ostende faciem, nàm ea salva ero.   662
        273 1   86   1   164   137
58.   Procùl à pœna, à culpa itidèm ;   662
        271   169   113   109
59.   Ultrà dolore haùd angar ;   662
        1   25   126   220   290
60.   A mè, Nate, abscedent mœrores,   662

61. Jàm plenè Cœlitibus lætior ; 662

62. Mihi ergò appare, redi, redde Tè mihi, 662

63. Nàm ità mihi bis JESUS fies. 662

JOSEPHUS MAZZA.

LUC. xi. 4.		PER CAB. ORD.	
Libera nos a malo.	399	Sine maculâ.	399
		Virgo fidelis.	399

LUC. xi. 27.		PER CAB. ORD.	
Benedicta sint ubera tua.	997	O Cœlum animatum.	997

JOHN i. 47.
PROG.

CABALA SIMPLEX 443 ET
CHRONOGRAMMA 1717.
(*Luther's Jubilee.*)

SIehe	40	DoCtor	71
EIn Wahrer	96	MartInVs	109
IsraeLIter	111	LVther	80
In DeM	43	gebohren	71
KeIn	37	zV	44
FaLsChes ist	116	EIssLeben	68
	443		443

J. F. RIEDERER.

JOHN xiv. 6.	PER CAB. ORD. 1696.
Tu mihi via et veritas et vita. 1696	Sacrosanctum Christi Corpus.

J. BLANCHINUS,
Single sheet folio, Romæ, 1696.

Heb. xii. 22.		Per Cab. ord.	
Jerusalem cęlestis.	762	Integra Jesu Mater.	762
		San Juan.	

John xix. 30.
Soliloquium.

	222	158	213	428	

INCLINATO CAPITE EMISIT SPIRITUM   1021

290 285 95 66 34 193 58
1. Exanimem igitùr Tè hodiè Filj videre debebo?   1021

4 117 116 332 92 105 255
2. Ac licèt sanè innocuum, sic deflere occisum?   1021

48 98 245 411 219
3. Oh Dies pessima, nefastissima omnium!   1021

48 202 90 168 99 414
4. Oh Meridies penè nocte omni obscurior!   1021

4 207 281 88 441
5. Ac læthæis umbris dirè tenebrosior!   1021

33 159 155 115 237 322
6. Hèm etenìm Solem omnem deliquio obfuscat,   1021

485 150 30 120 236
7. Æternumquè tandèm jàm addicit Occasui.   1021

95 35 48 180 95 181 89 298
8. Et en oh quali, et quàm immani sævitiæ,   1021

290 58 516 157
9. Quòt, ideò quibusquè plagis?   1021

159 39 129 150 280 264
10. Nedùm in Deum tandèm ausit impietas: 1021

235 110 212 464
11. Factorem nempè ingratè destruens,   1021

329 204 47 125 75 241
12. Auctorem Vitæ Neci etiàm infami adjudicans,   1021

69 417 291 244
13. Imò Salvatorem impijssimè perdens,   1021

89 190 104 368 270
14. Sèd ut modò desæviret acerbiùs: 1021

298 50 228 445
15. (Sævitiæ hinc cuilibet inexæquanda)   1021

16   179   159   282   385

16. Eccè plagens nulli pepercit cruciatui,   1021

100   240   124   320   237

17. Non ullum sinè vulnere Membrum :   1021

35   276   95   308   307

18. En ubiquè, et undiquè Sanguis ;   1021

185   100   50   174   123   389

19. Quem plenè Flagella, Spinæ, Clavi eduxere.   1021

48   125   30   447   137   125   109

20. Indè etiam jàm speciosus forma prę alijs,   1021

184   137   83   136   323   158

21. Jurè itidèm Campi Flos, Convallium Lilium,   1021

100   480   100   122   219

22. Non Vultus, non decor simùl,   1021

89   310   229   95   298

23. Sèd solus livor, & horror,   1021

51   100   339   89   24   418

24. Nàm non spectabilis, sèd Facie spectrum,   1021

129   20   159   69   323   321

25. Delicijs hic cares, imò horrorem incutis ;   1021

15   30   62   95   323   496

26. Ejà jàm Angeli Tè videntes horrescunt,   1021

258   149   1   340   100   173

27. Depulsi demùm à deformitate, non Radijs,   1021

30   160   146   228   222   235

28. Jàm ipsam tamèn nonnisi peramarè deflentes.   1021

293   16   118   140   214   64   176

29. Cæterùm eccè illis major inest flendi occasio :   1021

98   96   92   210   340   185

30. Homicidæ planè cædere debuit Summum Numen,   1021

38   100   96   432   355

31. Nèc non planè latronibus posthaberi :   1021

30   83   147   118   39   238   366

32. Jàm Barabbæ Plebs ignara in collatione posthabet,   1021

95   57   216   297   95   261

33. Et deindè Carnifices Iniquis Tè præhabent :   1021

108   106   201   432   174

34. Ceù latè fores latronibus pejor,   1021

115   361   244   4   297

35. Vèl latronum Caput, àc Princeps,   1021

33 39 235   78   30   606
36. Hèm in eorum medio jàm constitueris :   1021

33 125 109   284   470
37. Hèm prę alijs acerbissimè tortus.   1021

139   250   256   36   340
38. Aceto solùm, atquè Felle potaris,   1021

173   283   100   465
39. Cachinnis, convicijs ità vexaris,   1021

190 169   4   269   20   149   220
40. Ut dolore, àc pudore hic demùm depereas.   1021

4 95 92   330   27   62   169 100 142
41. Ac Tè sic perempto Cœli Angeli, qui non fleant   1021

89 36   382   514
42. Si malè corruit Universum !   1021

163   90   503   265
43. Nùnc ampli corruunt Montes,   1021

50 3 118   555   295
44. Adeò ab imis discutitur Tellus,   1021

130 144   242   505
45. Sol ipse condolens obtenebratur,   1021

140 125 221   243   292
46. Ipsa etiàm tota languet Natura,   1021

675   66   90   190
47. Empyreumvè hodiè penè mœret.   1021

131 52 186   180   193   100   179
48. Sola ego Mater verè langueo, non depereo :   1021

113   304   289   46   160   109
49. Heù : planctum Unigeniti mihi cogor efficere,   1021

124 30 95 323   228   95   126
50. Dùm jàm Tè viduor, nonnisi Tè habens !   1021

310 85   287   339
51. Unus es, Unicôvè privor :   1021

95   210   116 249 38 64   249
52. Et mœrens adhùc vivo, nèc enim morior   1021

250   110   202   190 269
53. Utinàm Tibi commori Matri detur :   1021

5 5 25 20   259   95 254   358
54. Dà, dà me hic defunctam Tè sequi defunctum ;   1021

181   164 96   169 100 311
55. Quam dolor planè immanis non obruit,   1021

149 123 261 213 275
56. Demùm Clavi, Cruces perdirè perimant : 1021

340 90 282 309
57. Totum penè Sanguinem effudisti, 1021

58 100 340 242 95 186
58. Ideò plenè totum effundat et Mater ; 1021

36 163 136 110 133 443
59. Fiam nùnc occisa Tibi simile Adjutorium ; 1021

36 115 234 636
60. Fiam vèl meritò Corredemptrix ; 1021

15 14 89 257 129 283 234
61. Ejà addè : si vivificam vim Cruor induat, 1021

260 215 27 298 9 176 36
62. Mòx admirabilis Cœli Pellicanus dè Columba fiam, 1021

179 205 65 262 200 110
63. Denuò ex meo Sanguine Vita Tibi. 1021

JOSEPHUS MAZZA.

JOHN xix. 34.
SOLILOQUIUM.

310 258 50 281 194 325
UNUS MILITUM LANCEA LATUS EJUS APERUIT. 1418

168 122 116 39 440 293 240
1. Pròh nefas ! adhùc in Mortuum desævit Barbaries ? 1418

4 204 204 93 347 372 194
2. Ac quod intèr largè horrendiora crudelitas redigit, 1418

204 95 408 100 255 356
3. Quòd et Atrociores plenè solent horrescere, 1418

104 39 95 129 115 358 30 548
4. Modò in Tè Deum vèl Defunctum jàm exercetur ! 1418

124 270 328 84 562 50
5. Dùm exanime Pectus dira transfigitur Lancea. 1418

58 125 225 206 271 533
6. Ideò etiàm arcaniora Cordis penetralia terebrantur. 1418

200 191 29 194 50 315 276 163
7. Vita tua, mi JESU, adeò cunctis habetur odibilis, 1418

190 159 30 385 97 280 43 234
8. Ut nedùm jàm auserint Impij acerbissima Nece perimere, 1418

89 95 115 113   204   42   272   204   284
9. Sèd et vèl Cor, quod benè fuerat Vitæ Radix   1418

49   266   661   442
10. Jò Feralitèr expungitur, dissecatur.   ·   1418

48   260   190   170 · 200   34   311   205
11. Oh Immanitas visa nullibi, nequè Filj unquàm audita !   1418

48   372   115 155   323   90   315
12. Oh crudelitas, vèl apud Tartara penè insueta !   1418

20 64   97   548   325   218   146
13. Ibi enìm efferè plectuntur Sontes, vivi tamèn :   1418

20 190 115 409   104   50   228 39   263
14. Hic Tù, vel functus, modò Lancea plagaris in Pectore,   1418

250 ·20 113   389   89 124   320   113
15. Quasi hic haud sævirent, si sine vulnere Cor.   1418

115 128 133 30   445   6   50   511
16. Vèl nisi illud jàm emortuum ea Lancea vulnerarent   1418

179 95   167   95   163   302   248   169
17. Novi, et probè, Tè nunc transfigi absque dolore,   1418

39 270   146   81   420   133 36   293
18. In Matris tamèn Animam vulnus illud malè desævit   1418

33   30 230 192   126   136   260   411
19. Hèm illa tuo divino Cordi Amore summo conglutinata,   1418

111 144 222   356   420   165
20. Ubi Ipse ictum excipis, vulnus accipit ;   1418

95 50 48 180   113   321   442   169
21. Et hinc oh quali, heù quanto urgetur dolore !   1418

181   570   150   148   50   319
22. Quàm extremus tandèm angor Illam invasit !   ·   1418

6 64 50   406   625   267
23. Ea enim hinc angustijs torquetur acerrimis,   1418

38 97   311   590   382
24. Nèc his unquàm substinuit graviores ;   1418

378 85 93 5   315   5   347   190
25. Sævities sè impiè, ad insueta, ad horrendiora redegit :   1418

96   65   290   · 233   170 104   136   95   229
26. Planè Animæ merores, angores, esse modò debent, et summi. 1418

219 122 204 30 390   282   171
27. Mirùm ergò quod Illa perstet Corpori colligata,   1418

38 190 85 1   355   325 1 109   314
28. Nèc, ut sè à doloribus eximat, à carne aufugiat ;   1418

324   295   204 25 5   63   100   305   97
29. Mirùmvè paritèr, quod Mè àd necem non perfodiant Impij, 1418

95 106 263   154 100 219   275   206
30. Et altè odientes Filium non simùl perimant Matrem ;   1418

254 180 220 62 185 122   194   26 175
31. Siquæ adest tanti odij causa, credo JESU, Mea est,   1418

39 25 122 88   261   123   54   316   390
32. In mè ergò diræ Cruces, Clavi, Lanceæ, Vulnera dirigantur ; 1418

174 116 92   239   262   535
33. Erit sanè longè minùs criminosa transfixio,   1418

38 270   372   50   688
34. Nèc voto crudelitas adeò frustrabitur ;   1418

161 89 230   448   245   245
35. Qua, si vivam percutiant, mortem inferent ;   1418

48 260 130 316   47   286   95 236
36. Indè, post Nati funus, neci addicetur et Parens.   1418

211 190 263   260   244   250
37. Fortè ut acriùs crucier, intactam tenent,   1418

30 25 1   428   40   273   71   99   451
38. Jàm mè à prænũciato almi Simeonis Gladio enecandã reservãt 1418

95 228 164 66 46 170 117   204 4   324
39. Et nonnisi dolor hodiè mihi esse debebit Ensis, ac Carnifex, 1418

95 144 81   115 259   145 1 65   122   391
40. Et ipse Animam, vèl invitam, coget à meo Corde exulare.   1418

91 190 61   26 173 92   411   39 335
41. At Tù, Anima mea, quid sic obstinaris in nexu ?   1418

15 310   372   200 282 239
42. Ejà resque vinculum, quo Corpori colligaris,   1418

9   245 211   338   194   50 219 152
43. Ah : rumpe moras, disrumpe nodum, hinc aufuge, avola !   1418

50   310 1 161 27   185   436 39 209
44. Hinc amissum à nobis Cœli Numen quæramus in Inferis: 1418

41   259   49 100 150 49   160   191   419
45. Illic Ipsum nil ità pati, nil despici, aùt pessumdari,   1418

89   329   59   411   281   249
46. Sèd videbimus inibi Tartaris omnibus Dominantem :   1418

69   59   1   326   243   117   203   3   202   195
47. Imò inibi à Reprobis, invitè licet, timeri, àb Electis adorari.   1418

173   122   386   20   61   4 45 173 30   100   304
48. Cùr ergò cunctaris hic Anima ? ac eò cùr jàm non convolas ? 1418

38   300   88   285   355   3   51   122   176
49. Nèc tantis dirè sauciata doloribus ab hoc Corde recedis ?   1418

102   227   320   65   392   47   265
50. Amas forsàn Unigenito meo diutiùs angi, cruciari,   1418

4   225   211   99   225   350   304
51. Ac dilectionem tuam omni morte fortiorem exhibere,   1418

165   125   34 130   309   481   174
52. Quæ etiàm mei Nati desunt passionibus, adimplere ?   1418

5   16   227 89   66   306   89   218 89   313
53. Ad hæc cuncta si hodiè respicis, si tendis, si ordinaris   1418

9   181   190 173 113   300   38 1   122   164   127
54. Ah permane, ut dolori Cor vivat, nèc à Corde dolor deficiat, 1418

199   140   349   24   272   252   182
55. Quin major duratione, fidè permaneat, crescat gradu.   1418

122 106 9   34   106 190   392   95   109   160 95
56. Ergò fiat, ah Filj, fiat ut diutiùs Tè, angar prò Tè ;   1418

190   131   100   233   164   25   330   245
57. Ut Amor plenè vincat, dolor mè nullus perimat   1418

15 190 191   360   260   1   49   352
58. Ejà ut tua adimpleatur Passio à Deo assumar.   1418

5   340   211   18   88   16   25   245   470
59. Ad summum decoris Dei apicem hæc mè tollet Assumptio :   1418

240   181   9   411   6   9   295   267
60. Plùs quàm dè Maternitate, ea dè Passione glorificabor,   1418

4   169   13   338   190 291   413
61. Ac dolens id adyciam, at citiùs resurgas :   1418

48   622   164   4 48   260   1 25 20   147   79
62. Oh inclytus Dolor, ac oh Passio à mè hic unicè diligenda !   1418

220   105   220 52   166   233   125 27   210   60
63. Vos amodò, tanti ego conscia pretij, prę Cœli Gaudijs diligam. 1418

JOSEPHUS MAZZA.

JOHN xx. 29.		PER CAB. TRIG.	
Dieweil	427	Herr Doctor	926
du mich	385	Michael	247
gesehen hast	769	Thomas	581
Thoma	410	Hochberümbter	1003
so glaubstu:	1155	Advocatus	904
Selig sind	642	zu	510
die nicht sehen	766	Leipzig	619
und doch glauben	882	in Patria	646
	5436		5436

J. F. RIEDERER.

ACTS ii. 36.		PER CAB. TRIG.	
So wisse	909	Der	178
nun das	574	Wohlehrenveste	1349
gantze Hauss	853	Vorachtbare	873
Israel	451	und	311
gewiss	490	Hochgelehrte	701
dass Gott	695	Herr	357
diesen Jesum	866	Johann Jacob	529
den ihr	350	Schudt	623
gekreuziget	1054	des	196
habt	230	Gymnasii	735
zu einem	754	zu Franckfurt	1411
Herrn und Christ	1360	hochverdienter	1080
gemacht hat	581	Corrector	824
	9167		9167

J. F. RIEDERER.

ACTS xiii. 25.

Als aber er seinen Lauff erfüllete sprache er: Ich bin nicht der, dafür ihr mich haltet.

PER CAB. TRIG.

Herr Gottfried Arnold von Annaberg gebürtig, Pastor zu Perlberg.

Acts xviii. 24, 25.

Ein beredter Mann, und mächtig
in der Schrifft, dieser war unter-
weisen den Weg des Herrn, und
redet mit brünstigem Geist, und
lehret mit Fleiss von dem Herrn.

10,586

Per Cab. Trig.

Herr Wolffgang Christoph. Desler,
berühmter Conrector der Schule
zum heiligen Geist, im neuen
Spital in der Keyserlich-freyen
Reichs-Stadt Nürenberg.   10,586

Acts xviii. 28.

Denn er	375
Überwande	729
die Juden	441
beständiglich	707
und erweisete	1161
öffentlich	590
durch	415
die Schrifft	713
dass Jesus	794
der Christ	785
seye	477
	7187

Per Cab. Trig.

Herr	357
Johann Jacob	529
Schudt	623
des	196
wohllöblichen	871
Gymnasii	735
zu	510
Franckfurth	937
am Mayn	525
hochverdienter	1080
Conrector	824
	7187

Acts xxvi. 28, 29.

Es fehlet nicht viel du überredest
mich dass ich ein Christ würde.
Er aber sprach : Ich wünschte vor
Gott es fehlet an viel oder wenig
dass nicht allein du, sondern Alle
die mich heute hören solche würden
wie ich bin.   13,211

Per Cab. Trig.

Herr Licentiatus Esras Edzardi ein
in Rabbinicis et Talmudicis sehr
hoch erfahrner Mann in Hamburg
gebohren anno 1629 xxviii Junii
starb anno 1708 1 Januarii.

13,211

Rom. xi. 8.

Gott hat	740
ihnen gegeben	473
einen	257
erbitterten	1060
Geist.	449
Augen	345
dass sie	413
nicht sehn	681
und Ohren	711
dass sie	681
nicht hören	768
biss auff	472
den heutigen Tag	920
	7702

Per Cab. Trig.

Herr Joannes Jacobus	1417
Schudtius	1049
Wolverdienter	1299
Rector	622
des löblichen	644
Gymnasii	735
zu Franckfurt	1411
am Mayn	525
	7702

1 Cor. xv. 22.

Omnes in Adam peccaverunt. 997

Per Cab. ord.

Non Mater Dei dulcissima et amabilis. 997
Non Tutelaris Hesperie. 997
Non enim immaculatissima Deipara. 997
Non enim Civitatis Dei Letitia. 997
Agna, munda, immunis a labe originali. 997
Pura a lue Adami, dona nobis pacem. 997
En Rosa virginea et munda. 997
Insignis Maria, ignorat maculam Ade. 997
O Cœlum vivum. 997
Omnia mea tua sunt. 997
Benedicta sint ubera tua. 997
Melliflua Maria munda malo Evæ. 997

San Juan.

1 Cor. iv. 11.

Biss auff diese Stund leiden wir Hunger und Durst und sind nacket und werden geschlagen und haben keine gewisse Stätte.   8029

Per Cab. Trig.

Die Zigauner ein verkappt nichts-würdiges liederliches Lumpen Volck von denen Frantzösen Egyptiens genannt.   8029

Col. i. 28.

Wir verkündigen Jesum, und ver-mahnen alle Menschen, und lehren alle Menschen mit aller Weisheit, auf dass wir darstellen einen jeglichen Menschen vollkoṁen in Christo Jesu.   11,103

Per Cab. Trig.

Der Ehrwürdig, Vorachtbar und Wohlgelahrte Herr Christian Hirsch verordneter Seelsorger und Archi–Diaconus in dem Nürnberg-ischen Städtlein Herrspruck.

          11,103

    J. F. Riederer.

Apoc. xii. 1.

Mulier amicta sole.   653

Per Cab. ord.

Liber signatus.   653
Gloriosa Virgo.   653
Cęlestis Sponsa.   653

    San Juan.

Apoc. xii. 1.

Luna sub pedibus ejus (Apoc. xii. 1).
Non dabit lumen suum (Matt. xxiv. 29).   2288

Per Cab. ord.

Leopoldus Imperator Germaniæ et Archidux Austriæ.   2288

Vienna plausus.

Apoc. xii. 1.

In capite ejus corona stellarum duodecim.   1606
Sol et Luna sub Pedibus ejus. 1491

Per Cab. ord.

Rubus ardens incombustus.   1606

Regina cui se cęlum et terra subjicit.   1491

    San Juan.

Apoc. xii. 3.

Ecce Draco Magnus, rufus, habens capita septem.   376

Cabala 376 Simplex.

Emericus Teccli, Hæreticus, re-bellis Cæsari.

Vienna plausus.

Apoc. xiv. 6.	Cabala 819 Simplex.
Ich sahe einen Engel fliegen mitten durch den Himmel der hatte ein ewig Evangelium zu verkündigen. 819	Martin Luther, Doctor in der heiligen Schrifft gebohren zu Eissleben, getauffet am Tage Martini. J. F. Riederer.

Apoc. xiv. 14.	Per Cab. ord.
Corona aurea super caput ejus. 1613	O Vita quæ contra mortem se nobis dedit. 1613 San Juan.

Apoc. xviii. 7.	Per Cab. Trig.
Denn sie spricht in ihrem Hertzen : Ich sitze und bin eine Königin und werde keine Wittib seyn und Leid werde ich nicht sehen. 7806	Her Sacred and Royal Majesty Anne, by the grace of God Almigty (*sic*) Queen of Great Britain, Scotland, France and Irland (*sic*), Defender of the Faith. 7806 J. F. Riederer.

J. F. Riederer generally adds some explanatory short poem to his cabala. In this instance it may be worth reproduction. The cabalist was a keen observer of the political world, clearly :—

Was kommt aus Engelland ? was hört man nun von Annen ?
Sie will dem Kayser jetzt zu hoch die Seyten spannen
Sie ändert ihren Sinn zu Windsor auf dem Schloss
Und König Ludwig wird ihr neuer Bundsgenoss.
Gedult ! Er wird gewiss euch unbestand'gen Britten
Die Langen auf den Kopff zu euren Schaden schütten ;
Nun gehts noch alles an, nun schläffert er euch ein,
Duc d'Aumont muste mehr als ein Verschwender seyn.
Der König mächts subtil, und kunt mit Lust erfinden
Das Kunst-stück, wie man euch könn ohne messer schinden.
Dem denck, O Anna, nach, du merckst die Brillen nicht,
Weh diesem blinden Volck, das Treu und Glauben bricht !

APPENDIX CABALISTICA.

DE APOSTOLIS ET SANCTIS.

Sanctus Paulus.	1095	De lupo Diaboli Cęlestis Agnus.	
			1095
Sanctus Lucas.	838	Est Pictor Medicus.	838
Sanctus Andreas.	745	In cruce gentes edoceas.	745
Sanctus Marcus.	928	Rugiens, pacem enunciat.	928
Sanctus Thomas.	803	Quia vidit, credit.	803
Sanctus Joannes Evangelista.	1237	Ego ut Aquila Divina Solis amica.	
			1237
Sanctus Thadæus.	933	O Frater Jhesu Christi.	933
Sanctus Simon.	743	De pio zelo ardeo.	743
Sanctus Stephanus.	1115	Ille Fidei Prothomartyr.	1115
Sanctus Joseph.	746	Mariæ Sponsus.	746
Sancta Anna.	317	Dei filiam habe, Adæ sine labe.	317

Omnes Sancti et Sanctæ Dei.	821
O Cœlestis Hierusalem.	821

Sancta Maria Virgo.	702	Hæc carens Evæ macula.	702
Sancta Maria.	356	Longe a peccato Adæ.	356
		Pia Dei Mater Alma.	356
		O Hæc Cœli Janua.	356
		Ego Dei Parens.	356
		Ego electa Sol.	356
		Ego facta sine labe Adæ.	356
		Ego innocens Dei Filia.	356
		Ea illibata a crimine Adæ.	356

PENTAMETRUM ET CABALISTICUM.

Ecce ea Filia Adæ, Mater amica
Dei.   356

The following elegiacs are highly ingenious, being formed wholly from the *cabalistica* of the names of our Saviour—viz., JESUS CHRISTUS = 974, and JHESUS CHRISTUS = 982, of which a further series is given lower down.

Disticha.

Hex. et Pen.

Filius hic Mariæ Deus est | Sanctus Benedictus.
974   982

Solus Dux hic | cor abstulit ille meum.
974   974

Naturæ lege es Dominus | mihi servus amore es.
982   982

Orbis sum cæli Rex | ego sum quia sum.
974   982

| Jesu. | 304 | Sancta Maria. | 356 |
| Miserere. | 304 | Ora pro me. | 356 |

Jesus Maria.   515
Meum cor ; anima mea.

| 402 | Jhesus | Maria. | 121 |
| 402 | Ac meum cor | ac anima mea. | 121 |

Jesus et Maria.   620
Sol est, ac Luna.   620

Giesù.	311	Maria.	121
Benedetto.	311	Anima mea.	121
Amante dell' anime.	311	E mia gioia.	121

JESUS CHRISTUS.	974
Iste Filius Dei vivi.	974
O una et vera bonitas.	974
Es Deus per quem omnia.	974
Dominus Deus Sabaoth.	974
Solus Sanctus.	974

HEXAMETRUM AND CABALISTICON.

HEXAMETRA AND CABALISTICA.

JESUS.	394	JHESUS.	402
Do Vitam.	394	Salvas.	402
Hic Carus.	394	Hic bonus.	402
Es panis esca.	394	O Dei Filius.	402
Cor ines anima mea.	394	O Victima.	402
		Cordi Amor es.	402

All above in this appendix are by Joannes Evangelista à Panormo,* and all by ordinary cabala :—

1	2	3	4	5	6	7	8	9	10	20	30	40	50	60	70	80	90
A	B	C	D	E	F	G	H	I	K	L	M	N	O	P	Q	R	S

100	200	300	400	500
T	U	X	Y	Z

A good one by Cabala Simplex is :—

$$\overset{38}{\text{Maria}}\ \overset{64}{\text{Virgo.}}\qquad 102$$

$$\overset{41}{\text{Sola}}\ \overset{43}{\text{sine}}\ \overset{18}{\text{labe.}}\qquad 102$$

SIGISMUNDO À S. SYLVERIO,
Prælusiones Poeticæ.

HEBREW CABALISTICA ON THE NAME OF JESUS
(IN HEBREW, JESCHUA).
PER GEMATRIAM 386.

JESUS.	386
He is sent from God.	386
He is the forgiveness of sins.	386
The Redeemer ; the son of Mary.	386
He will make free.	386
He is God, Creator of the world.	386
He is Man and God.	386

* See Bibliography.

He shall reign on high.   386
The wisdom of God.   386
He is the Light of the World.   386
King of the whole earth.   386
Before the world existed, He was.   386
He is the Son of Almighty God.   386
Jehovah is His Father's Name.   386
And He is Man from Mary.   386
His name is the Redeemer.   386
With His Blood hath He redeemed.   386
He is the Redeemer from the power of the wicked enemy.   386
He is merciful and gracious.   386

ELCHANON PAULUS,
Pragensis.

APPENDIX

CABALISTIC CURIOS,
SCRIPTURAL, PATRISTIC, AND LUTHERAN

APPENDIX

CABALISTIC CURIOS,

SCRIPTURAL, PATRISTIC, AND LUTHERAN

$$\boxed{153}$$

THE FISHES DRAWN TO LAND BY SIMON PETER.

THIS odd number has been much discussed both theologically and cabalistically. The theological question was somewhat settled by the great authority of St. Augustine and other Fathers long ago.

They saw in 153 a proof of the fact that the number of the elect is fixed and pre-ordained.

No large indefinite number is given to us in the miracle, but a small certain and particular one.

The cabalistical solution of this has been often attempted, and many fantastic and obviously absurd solutions have been offered. Lately, however, more reasonable views seem coming to the front, and some progress is being made in a more likely direction. People who are open to reason and conviction will not be so ready now to pronounce unreservedly that the Biblical cabala is utter nonsense, or on a par with Donnelly's cryptogram.

The assumption is that 153 is cabalistically the number of the Sons of God.

This expression, "Sons of God" (*Beni ha-Elohim*), occurs several times in Scripture, and *per gematriam* it counts up 153. In Greek the expression exhibits in another form the same phenomena, the gematria being 3213 or 3 × 7 × 153.

In Job ii. 1 is this remarkable cabala, *Beni ha-Elohim*, with Satan among them, which counts up altogether 1989, and the two factors of this are 153 and 13, 1989 = 13 × 153, 13 being the mark of the adversary.

In Rom. viii. 17 we have συνκληρονόμοι (joint heirs) = 1071 = 7 × 153 ; also κτίσις θεοῦ (the creation of God) = 1224 = 8 × 153.

In the records of the miracle itself there are some remarkable cabalistic coincidences.

The word for fishes is ἰχθύες = 1224 = 8 × 153, and the words for the net are τὸ δίκτυον, which also by gematria = 1224 = 8 × 153, both rightly numbers of perfection and regeneration, for the net is unbroken, and carries the precious freight from the " right side " of the ship safely to the shore, and " not one is lost."   Moreover, this word ἰχθύες (fishes) is exactly value for the same 1224 in the name of Abram, to whose seed, through Ephraim and Manasses, the promise was made that they should increase as fishes do increase.

Thus there is established a remarkable numerical connection between the seed of the patriarch and God's chosen people, whether we consider them metaphorically as fishes or as the actual people whom God through His prophet addresses as " My people, the house of Israel."

We read in Ezekiel xxxiv. 30, " Thus shall they know that I the Lord their God am with them, and that they, even *the house of Israel, are my people*, saith the Lord God."   And the Greek words " house of Israel, My people " = 1530 = 10 × 153, where we see the *Ten* Tribes marked out.

Also " Mary and Jesus," that is, the woman and her seed = 1071 = 7 × 153 ; and " the seed of Jacob " in Hebrew = 459 = 3 × 153. And when the net was drawn to land Jesus strictly enjoined Peter to " Feed my *sheep*," a term used throughout the Bible to designate God's people, the house of Israel.

There is another way in which this peculiar number 153 has been regarded, and is perhaps worth considering here.

The division of the year into 7 months for the " Seed," and 5 months for the " Fish," as types of the Resurrection, both as found in the Gospels and in the history of Noah and the Flood, is distinctly marked out in the Divine system of number. 153 is the number of the *fishes* in John xxi. 11, and 207 is the number of days that formed the Jewish ritual, the *seed*-ripening period. The sum of these two numbers is 360, the number of the year. The division of the number 360 at the Flood is, it is true, slightly different; for there is 150 days for the fish period, leaving 210 for the period when the sun is triumphant.

But in either case there are 5 signs for the one period and 7 for the other. Perhaps the idea is to show not only the division into 7 signs and 5, but to bring out that 3 day-and-nights, *nychthemera*, at the Vernal Equinox, occupy a peculiar position, being the period that links the "Fish" period on to the "Seed" period, the cross of the ecliptic and equator occurring at the 14th to 17th Nisan, when the Ark, ceasing to float, rested.*

Hengstenberg found in this number the fulness of the Gentiles indicated according to 2 Chron. ii. 17, where Solomon reckons the strangers in Israel at 153,600. They had toiled all night on unproductive toil in Israel, and now the Light of Day shall begin to rise and spread o'er all the earth, and the Gentiles shall walk in it.

Dr. Egli (*Theol. Jahr.*, 1854, p. 135) finds the number in Simon Peter's name, *i.e.*, Shimeon Jonah = 153.

153 is a remarkable number in many ways. $153 = 1^3 + 5^3 + 3^3 = $ the sum of its separate cubes; $153 = 17 \times 3^2$; also $153 = 1 + 2 + 3 + 4 \ldots + 17$, the sum of the first 17 numbers.

Now, 17 is the *seventh* of the series of prime numbers, 1, 3, 5, 7, 11, 13, 17, etc., and 13 is the *sixth* of the same series. Hence, while 17 is connected with 7, 13 is connected with 6. Now 7 is admitted on all hands to be Biblically significant of spiritual perfection, and 6 is the number Biblically significant of imperfection, labour, and opposition, and as we know how remarkably 13 is indicated as the number of opposition in the Bible, we may take it that 17 represents spiritual perfection, and, moreover, the fact of its being a combination of 7 + 10, the numbers of spiritual perfection, helps our assumption.

* *The Computation of* 666 (London, 1891, 8vo), at p. 244. For further exposition see chap. vi., "The Fish and the Seed of Corn."

Petrus Bungus, who wrote in the sixteenth century a ponderous work on numbers, has a few good remarks on 153. He endeavours, as his title-page expresses it, to show a wondrous and unceasing agreement between the old Pythagorean principle of mystic numbers and the principle of numeration used frequently in the Holy Scriptures. Necessarily there is much that is pure fancy in so elaborate a work, but he had carefully gone to all the original sources open to him at the time, and so his book is not without a certain value still. He says that the 153 fishes signify the whole multitude of the elect who shall be on the right hand of the Throne on the Day of Judgment.

It was shortly after our Lord's Resurrection that the wonderful draught of fishes is related, and therein was a reference to the resurrection to a new and eternal life for all who were safely brought " out of the deep " into the ship or ark of the Church which floats at peace on the troubled and rising waters. The net was cast on the right side of the ship ; therefore there were no reprobate sinners taken in the net, for all these were on the left side. The net was not broken ; heresy and schism had not yet done damage. As for 153, it is the trigonal number of 17, and 17 represents the man complete in Christ, who has been purified like silver *seven* times from his native dross, and has received his *denarius*, *i.e.*, his 10 and his 7.

" And do you wish to know yet further," he adds, " why the whole number of the saints is denoted by 17 ? Then take this reason as well. What is the peculiar number of the Law of Moses ? How many are the Commandments ? Are they not 10 ? But the Law, if it be not helped by Grace, leaves men in their trespasses and sins, and is the Letter only. And so the Apostle pointedly says, The Letter killeth, but the Spirit maketh alive."

The result therefore is, that we must add the Spirit to the Letter, and perform the precepts of the Law in and through the Grace of our Saviour. This is adding 7 to 10 cabalistically, and the number of the perfect Christian (17) comes out, and, rising *per cab. trigonalem* 1 + 2 + 3 . . . 17 to 153, represents the whole Church of the Elect and Perfect, which is the Body of Christ.*

* *Petri Bungi Bergomatis Numerorum Mysteria.* (Editio Lut. Paris., 1617, pp. 593-5.)

6 AND 666

6 may be considered cabalistically a 7 − 1—*i.e.*, man's coming short of spiritual perfection.

It has to do with MAN, as examination of many instances of its use seem convincingly to show. It is the human number, the number of Man, destitute of God.

Man was created on the 6th day; 6 days were appointed for him to labour, and the *seventh* day for spiritual rest with God.

Curiously enough, 6 seems stamped on much that has to do with human labour—it is stamped on his *measures*, so to speak—

$$1 \text{ foot} = 12 = 2 \times 6 \text{ inches,}$$
$$1 \text{ yard} = 36 = 6 \times 6 \text{ or } 6^2 \text{ inches,}$$

and on his time—

$$1 \text{ day} = 24 = 4 \times 6 \text{ hours,}$$
$$1 \text{ year} = 12 = 2 \times 6 \text{ months,}$$
$$1 \text{ hour} = 60 = 10 \times 6 \text{ minutes} = 100 \times 6 \times 6 \text{ seconds.}$$

If 6 cabalistically represents Man without God, we may well expect that 666, or the threefold 6, should represent still more essentially the same idea, and so we find it. The Edomites were essentially aliens from God and enemies of Israel, and the Biblical word for them is HADVMIM, and this word sums up into 666.

To mega therion—" the great beast "—also counts up 666.

The words *antitheos esti*—" he is Antigod "—also equal 666.

Again, there is one word in the New Testament (Acts xix. 25) which occurs only once—viz., *euporia*, meaning wealth, the ill-gotten gains of Demetrius the shrine-maker, and it numbers 666, and when we remember the many denunciations in the New Testament against riches, this seems a remarkable coincidence. And what is still more remarkable is that of the 3125 different nouns which the New Testament contains, this is the only one which counts up 666. In the Old Testament, too, there is a singular parallel, for in 1 Kings x. 14 we read : " Now the weight of gold that came to Solomon in one year was six hundred threescore and six talents of gold."

Indeed, wherever in Scripture this bestial number appears alone, the sense is usually a sinister one.   For instance, in that remarkable passage where our Lord's disciples express fear of shipwreck, the word is (Matt. viii. 25), "Lord, save us ; *we perish* ($\dot{a}\pi o\lambda\lambda\dot{v}\mu\epsilon\theta a$)," and this word equals 666, and probably is the only verb in the New Testament which exactly fits the number.

Then the slave or concubine offspring of Leah and Rachel also make up each 666, *per gematriam Hebraicam*, thus :—

Leah	36	Bilhah	42
Zilpah	122	Dan	54
Gad	7	Naphtali	570
Asher	501		
	666		666

The apostate Ham, if reckoned with his father Noah, becomes 666, while Noah and his two other sons, Shem and Japhet (omitting Ham), become 888, the number of the name of Jesus.

Again, Shechem Ben Hamor, who in his seduction of Dinah is said to prefigure the seduction of Israel by the Antichrist, counts up 666 in the most characteristic way, for Shechem gives 360, and Ben Hamor 306, the same division as in Nero Cæsar.

Again, there are three men who stand out in Scripture as avowed enemies of God and His people.   Each is branded with this number 6.

1. Goliath, whose height was 6 cubits, and he had 6 pieces of armour, and his spear's head weighed 600 shekels of iron.

2. Nebuchadnezzar, whose "image," which he set up, was 60 cubits high, and 6 cubits broad (Dan. iii. 1), and which was worshipped when the music was heard from 6 specified instruments.   Moreover, the words in Dan. iii. 1 equal by gematria 4662, which has the significant factors 7 × 666.

3. Antichrist, whose number is 666.

There are further significant peculiarities in 666, for besides its three sixes, it is the sum of the first 36 (*i.e.*, 6 × 6) numbers—viz., 1 + 2 + 3 up to 36, and also the sum of the only 6 numerical letters which the Romans used, as thus appears :—

1. D = 500
2. C = 100 } 600
3. L = 50
4. X = 10 } 60
5. V = 5
6. I = 1 } 6 } 666

1000 was represented by CIƆ, and later by **M**.

I will not burden my pages with the names of those many persons of both great and small reputations who have been marked by curious calculators with the bestial number of the Apocalypse. Personally, I am inclined to accept the very strong evidence that points to Nero Cæsar, but· there are other remarkably good conjectures which cannot be summarily put out of court. Different minds see evidence of this peculiar sort in very different lights, and as I have already remarked, the author * who has devoted the most time and the biggest book to the investigation of the hidden name passes by almost unnoticed that solution which historically and cabalistically seems to me the most ingenious and probable. So I leave this vexed question and present two rare and curious cabalistical exercises on 666—one from our early Lutheran friend, whom I have mentioned elsewhere, and the other from a mystical French writer of much more recent date.

666

Ecce Bestia Magna	666
Hæc habet Capita	666
Ac ibi Cornua	666
Eia ea septem	666
At diademata decem	666
Ac erunt	666
Regis iræ Dei	666
Ecce Belua ab Ecclesia	666
De eadem Babylon	666

* David Thom, Ph.D., M.A., *The Number and Names of the Apocalyptic Beast.* (London, 1848.)

Ea fit latina	666
Ecce ea fit Romæ	666
De illa Leones	666
De hac Leones ad decem	666
Illi decem de Belua	666
Abnegat Roma	666
Fidem ac acta filii dei	666
Hic cecidit fides	666
Et Ecclesia fidei	666
Sed Sodoma	666
Ac Gomorrha	666
Rhoma plena	666
Sed ecce Leo Papa	666
Ac os peccati	666
Id Bestia Leo	666
Hic vere Leo	666
Ac jam Decimus	666
Et in Ecclesia	666
Leo et Draco	666
Damnat Belua	666
Omnia Bulla	666
Damnat leges	666
Etiam pias	666
Dilectionem	666
Consilia fidei	666
Et fidem filii dei	666
Hæc fides cito	666
Efficit alieno	666
Alieno labore	666
Ope verbi	666
Bona æterna	666
Et vitæ	666
Eternæ, Amen	666
Væ Bestiæ	666

This is a fairly strong cabalistic marking out of Pope Leo Decimus as the "Beast," but our author goes further yet, and uses the mystic numbers of Daniel and St. John in such a way as to leave no doubt, for, as he says, no other Pope that ever lived could be so clearly marked:—

666 gives Id Bestia Leo.
1260 „ Et idem Leo, Leo Decimus.
1290 „ Iste idem Leo Decimus.
1335 „ Leo, Leo Papa, Leo Decimus.
666 and 1260 taken together give Papa Leo Decimus, Papa Leo Decimus.
1290 and 1335 give Et idem Papa Leo Decimus, Antichristus.

This certainly reads well, and seems without a flaw—straightforward and clear enough, anyhow. But he has more behind.

In Apoc. xvii. 5 we read of the woman sitting on the scarlet-coloured beast, and are told "upon her forehead was a name written : MYSTERY, BABYLON THE GREAT "—*i.e.*, in the Latin—

Mysterium in fronte Babylon Magna,

and this *per cabalam trigonalem* equals—

Nomen Papatus in fronte Leo Decimus.

But according to our author's theory, Leo X. was only one head of the Beast, for (Apoc. xvii. 10) there are seven heads and seven kings or Popes. So he goes to St. John again, and takes 666 + 666 + 1260 + 1260, which give by the same *cabala* used throughout :—

Fit Papa Adrianus Sextus, Papa Clemens Septimus (the next two Popes);

then 666 + 66 + 6 + 1290 + 1335 give—

Papa Paulus Tertius, Papa Julius Tertius (the next two Popes),

the last being alive when our author wrote, and so it began to look as if the times of the end were near. But we have much more of these Popes in the great cabalistic exposition of 1290 + 1335, Daniel's "last days "; the cabalistic number 2625.

A French Cabalisticon.

By *J. A. Soubira*,* published in a pamphlet of 4 pp., entitled "666," at Cahors in 1824.

L'Alphabet Numérique.

1	2	3	4	5	6	7	8	9	10	20	30	40	50	60	70	80	90
A	B	C	D	E	F	G	H	I	K	L	M	N	O	P	Q	R	S

100	110	120	240	130	140	150
T	U	V	W	X	Y	Z

Le 19me siècle hissera de l'orage	666
Son mondain zéphir,	666
En altérera le paysage	666
Et déracinera le visir.	666
Le 19me siècle dégradera le paganisme,	666
Fera mourir l'Alcoran,	666
Marteler le vandalisme	666
Et rogner le Vatican !	666
Ce siècle échenillera l'Europe	666
Afin de brider son ambition,	666
Et de bénir l'horoscope	666
Qui doit rafler Albion !	666
Ce siècle transira l'Asie	666
Annullera le stilet	666
Enchainera l'hypocrisie	666
Et réformera Mahomet !	666
Ce siècle échauffera l'Afrique	666
Tisonnera l'escroc,	666
Diffamera sa politique,	666
Et déchaussera le froc !	666

* Soubira, Jacob Abraham, notaire à Montcuq, arrondissement de Cahors, versificateur qui a pris successivement les titres de poëte d'Israël, d'émigré français en 1791, et de délégué du Messie. Querard (*La France Littéraire*, s.v.) gives titles of many of his works (48). They appear all to be small pamphlets of four, eight, sixteen, and twenty-four pages. "666": This pamphlet does not appear in the list.

Ce siècle retapera le N. Monde,	666
Et va régénérer Panama	666
Afin de régenter son onde	666
Et démettre son lama !	666
Ce 19me siècle enfin fera grandir la bible	666
Et rôtir le Geudas	666
Qui poignarde le paisible	666
Et dessèche ces climats !	666
Bref, la naïve prophétie	666
Qui fait figurer Gog *	666
Et régénérer le Messie	666
Écrasera bientôt Magog.†	666
Malgré son terrible Alcide Dobrowsky ‡	666
Adroit au charivari	666
En *ut, re, mi, fa, sol, la, si.*	666
Verra pâlir son égide.	666

8 AND 888

8 cabalistically considered was 7 + 1 ; something added to spiritual completeness, which is 7. Hence 8 is specially associated with Resurrection and Regeneration, and the beginning of a new era or order.

Ex.—Noah was the *eighth* person (2 Peter ii. 5) who was found in the ark to commence with a new order of things in a new birth, and 8 souls came out with him.

Circumcision on the 8th day, a sign of a new order or creation.

Christ rose from the dead on the first day of the week, which was, of course, the eighth day as well.

* Gog = le christianisme.
† Magog = le paganisme (Ézéch. xxxviii.).
‡ Il paraît actuellement à Astracan, *Un Journal de Musique asiatique*, par le Professeur de Musique Dobrowsky. Le *Diable à Quatre* déchu du privilège d'avoir le nombre 666 dans les lettres de son nom, reconnaît Dobrowsky pour son doyen et pour grand lama.—(Moncuq, 10 août, 1824, Soubira.)

The Feast of Tabernacles lasted 8 days, and is connected by John i. 14 with the Incarnation, for it is written: " The Word was made Flesh and *dwelt* among us," and *dwelt* is in the · original Greek ἐσκήνωσεν—*i.e.*, " tabernacled " among us.

It may well be called (as it has been) the Dominical Number, for it occurs constantly in connection with our Lord. It is the number of His name ΙΗΣΟΥΣ = 888, and it comes in a curious way into His other names as well—

Χριστός, Christ	=	1480	= 8 ×	185.
Κύριος, Lord	=	800	= 8 ×	100.
Κύριος ἡμῶν, Our Lord	=	1768	= 8 ×	221.
Σωτήρ, Saviour	=	1408	$= 8^2 ×$	22.
Ἐμμανουήλ, Emmanuel	=	25,600	$= 8^3 ×$	50.
Messias = Messiah	=	656	= 8 ×	82.

8 is the first cubic number, and there seems to be something of perfection indicated—something the length and breadth and height of which are equal. The Holy of Holies, both in the Tabernacle and in the Temple, were *cubes*—in the Tabernacle a cube of 10 cubits ; in the Temple of 20 cubits. In Rev. xxi. the New Jerusalem is to be a cube of 12,000 furlongs.

In the Bible the names of the Lord's people are marked by 8 and multiples of 8 in a most remarkable way, while the enemies of God and His people are similarly marked by the number 13 and its multiples.*

DANIEL AND HIS COMPANIONS.

DAN. i. 6.

These count up 888 :—

Daniel	95
Hananiah	120
Misael	381
Azariah	292
	888

* For this, see Bullinger's *Number in Scripture*, pp. 205–234, where there are full details.

In Ps. xxii. 31, David says of Christ, " They shall come, and shall declare His righteousness unto a people that shall be born." The Hebrew here sums up a total of 888. Jesus is also spoken of as " The salvation of Israel," and the words of the Septuagint (*e soteria Israel*) are equal to 2 × 888 exactly.

We know from Gen. xlix. that Shiloh is the name of Messias when he comes, and if we add " I am that I am " to Shiloh, we get 345 + 543, which equals 888, the number of Jesus.

Jesus said (John x. 7) : " Verily, verily, I say unto you, I am the door of the sheep." The sum of this quotation is 5120, which is an exact equivalent to ten times 8 × 8 × 8.

And again, that well-known text in Isaiah, " His name shall be called Wonderful, Counsellor, the Mighty God, the Everlasting Father, the Prince of Peace." These six words as they run in the Hebrew, and so correspond with the six letters in the name Jesus, also sum up precisely 888.

2300, 1335, 1290

In accordance with the promise of the Introduction, I give here a selection from the remarkable treatment of the mystic and prophetic numbers of Daniel, in which an early Lutheran cabalist indulged his genius. I have referred to him at p. 23.

I think his greatest success was with the number 2300 (Dan. viii. 14). This number is of itself rather a remarkable one, as we shall see in the succeeding exposition of it. It is a perfect pyramidal number, a *numerus trigonalis*, and is the sum of all the letters of the Latin alphabet when they have been numbered according to the triangular progression 1, 3, 6, 10 . . . 276, *i.e.*—

. .: .:. .::. etc.

I doubt whether any intellectual quality of mind save the plodding and unconquerable perseverance of a genuine German could have accomplished such a feat as the following, for we now have in succession the extraordinary number of 316 appropriate Latin lines which are, every one of them, pure and correct *cabalistica* of the difficult triangular kind, known as *cabala trigonalis*. Each Latin line, if reckoned up according to the numerical value of its letters, and according to triangular progression, will amount to 2300 exactly. What makes these 316 lines the more remarkable is the wonderful clearness and neatness of their sense as applied to the matter in hand.

2300.

Ista est summa summarum	2300
Summa summarum ex Alphabeto	2300
Ex Alphabeto latino fit Numeris	2300
Atque est Numerus Danielis	2300
Ecce summa sacra totius Alphabeti	2300
Summa audita a Daniele Danielis octavo	2300
Et est summa sacra de cœlo signata	2300
Ecce Numerus Triangulorum	2300
Triangulis complet Alphabetum	2300
Et ecce fit pyramis triangulata.	2300
Ecce hic Numerus est hoc Alphabetum	2300
Ecce hoc viginti tribus literis	2300
Et ex hoc numero computatio	2300
Ac computatio literis solis	2300
Solis numeris eisdem annexis.	2300
Ecce Alphabetum latinum et certum	2300
Alphabetum latinum in numeris	2300
Hæc ipsa puncta duo millia trecenta	2300
Perficiunt dies Antiochi Epiphanis	2300
Dies Antiochi ac puncta Alphabeti latini	2300
Ea indicant istam progressionem dei	2300
Progressio Computationum.	2300

So far this famous number 2300 is made to describe itself as the sum of all the letters of the Latin alphabet, twenty-three in number, from A to Z, reckoned up according to the numeration known as Trigonalis, or triangular, viz.—

.   .·   .·.   .·.·   A, B, C, D, etc.,

the number of the points being 2300, and the progressive computation was divinely chosen to denote the final period of Antiochus Epiphanes.

But this is by no means all.   The mystic 2300 is only a prefatory indicator of the other mystic pairs of numbers in Daniel and John— viz., 1290 and 1335 in Daniel, and 666 and 1260 in John.   This is shown by doubling 2300, and we get : 2300 + 2300 equals

Ecce 1290, 1335 ; ac 666, 1260,

and no other two words but *ecce* and *ac* will suit, so, as our old author says, he did not put them there, but found them there.

This certainly is an extraordinary cabalistical coincidence, however else we may regard it.   So, having found this, he proceeds to develop further these prophetical numbers out of his basic number 2300, by a further cabalistic examination of it.

Iste Numerus Danielis est a Deo	2300
Et est Liber Danielis sigillatus	2300
Est Prologus clausus a Deo	2300
Descriptus intus ac foris	2300
Ille prologus est latinus	2300
Est præfatio clausa et sigillata	2300
Et præfatio latina e latino Alphabeto	2300
Pater dixit latina mysteria	2300
De latina Ecclesia, De latino Antichristo	2300
Hoc est de Papa adversario Christi	2300
De Antichristo Papa pater dixit	2300
Et dixit septem Tonitrua	2300
Hæc filius, Hæc spiritus dixit,	2300
Hæc dixit Dominus omnipotens.	2300

Hæc verba domini dei non sunt amissa	2300
Nec dominus hæc frustra dixit	2300
Erant enim signata in Apocalypsi Dei	2300
Nec signa illorum sunt amissa	2300
Ecce duo 666 ac 1260	2300
In istis duobus numeris dei	2300
Erant, sed non fuerant scripta.	2300
Qui eorum intellectum habet a Deo	2300
Ille computet Tempus Ecclesiæ dei	2300
Computetque nomen ac acta Bestiæ	2300
Nomen signatum Bestiæ 666	2300
Et Numerum 1260	2300
Ipse computet ex Alphabeto latino	2300
Numerum Meretricis notabilem	2300
Ecce dies Antiochi clara figura Papatus	2300
Et dies malorum Antiochi Epiphanis	2300
Figura malorum Vicarii Christi	2300
Antiochus Epiphanes figura finis	2300
Est figura Antichristi Leonis	2300
Ecce revelabitur prope finem mundi	2300
Papatus Papæ, Papæ Antichristi.	2300
Inicium calculati Papatus, est	2300
Johannes Octavus 852	2300
Et ab eisdem Tempus Antichristi	2300
Antichristi regnantis incipit	2300
Anni Papatus et religio Ecclesiæ Papæ	2300
Regnat Meretrix cum sit Papa	2300
Atque Papatum orbis designat	2300
Ecce hæc Meretrix Meretrix Bestiæ	2300
Designata Meretrix maxima mundi	2300
Babylon magna Meretrix Papistica	2300
Ecce ipsa damnat fidem justificationis	2300
Sed revelabitur verbum domini	2300
Postea non proficient ultra	2300
Inimici Christi impiis Papæ legibus.	2300

Ecce Antichristus, Ecce Leo, Leo decimus	2300
Ecce iste Papa Urbis revelatur	2300
Et fit hoc anno sexto Leonis decimi	2300
Eo anno domini 1518	2300
Anni Antichristi sunt finiti	2300
Anni 666 plene sunt finiti	2300
Coepti ergo ab anno domini 852	2300
Evangelium Apostolicum domini dei	2300
Et lux fidei usque ad annum 228	2300
Et ecce ab eo sumpserunt inicium	2300
Operationes erroris aperte	2300
Coepti ergo anni et dies ablati sacrificii	2300
Et omnia tempora hæc sunt finita	2300
Aperte anno 1518.	2300
Est tunc finita dispersio magna	2300
Et facta est Ecclesia una et fidelissima	2300
Ab Angelo volante per medium cœli, habente	2300
Evangelium æternum gloriosi dei,	2300
Habente claritatem magnam verborum	2300
Ecce enim a gloria claritatis ipsius	2300
Illuminata est terra Ubique.	2300

So far for the cabalistical and prophetical evolution of John's two mystic numbers out of the 2300. Next for Daniel's two :—

Ecce verba in Daniele sic sunt sigillata	2300
Verba sigillata ac sermones clausi	2300
Clausi signatique sermones dei	2300
Et ecce numeri sunt sermones	2300
Numeri Danielis et Apocalypsis	2300
Hi numeri sunt numeri finis	2300
Sunt verba et Evangelium Filii dei	2300
Daniel audivit mysteria clausa	2300
Ecce eadem audivit Daniel in visione sua	2300
Audivit mysteria dei sigillata	2300

De Christo sancto sanctorum	2300
Audivit mysteria Paparum	2300
At hæc sunt verba latina sigillata	2300
Ideo vir dei Daniel illa non intellexit	2300
Et ecce dum Daniel quæreret et diceret	2300
Quid erit post illa tempora dei ?	2300
Quid erit quod modo dixisti?	2300
Dicebat Angelus. In fine dierum apparebis	2300
Vade jam mi Daniel ac esto jam quietus	2300
Quietus esto penitus	2300
Eadem enim signata sunt Numeris.	2300
Ecce sermones modo sunt clausi	2300
Et mysteria sunt signata	2300
Eadem mysteria sunt sigillata	2300
Ipsa mysteria de filio dei patris	2300
De Antichristo Papa et de abominatione	2300
Signata per numeros sunt	2300
Qui numeri revelabuntur.	2300
Mysterium revelationis	2300
Istud est in tempore suo	2300
Illud præteribunt plurimi	2300
Et pertransibunt tempora	2300
Tempora et signata mysteria	2300
Eos Numeros præteribunt	2300
Et præteribunt verba signata.	2300
Numeri dei sunt mysteria dei	2300
Mysteria dei sunt Tempora	2300
Tempora signata per Numeros	2300
Sunt sigilla verborum ac liber	2300
Liber domini ineffabiliter copiosus	2300
In eo sunt verba ultima Ecclesiæ Dei	2300
Ecce iste liber nunc est tuus.	2300
Hunc librum dierum obsignabis Daniel	2300
Habet verba et sermones latinos	2300

Et librum et sermones claude Daniel	2300
Sermones illi latini ac verba hæc latina	2300
Habent mysteria de Antichristo	2300
Mysteria latinorum clausa	2300
Signata sigillata ab illis numeris	2300
Scientia libri erit multiplex	2300
Multiplex scientia Lutheri	2300
Ipsa erit de filio dei Ihesu Christo	2300
Et de illa Antithesi Christi et Papæ	2300
Signata illis sacris numeris dei	2300
In Numeris dei est Antithesis	2300
Antithesis sermonum domini dei.	2300
Hæc omnia omnes impii non intelligent	2300
Proficient in pejus donec pereant	2300
In termino mundi pessimè deficient	2300
Verba aperta de filio dei non videbunt	2300
Nec intelligent mysteria Bestiæ	2300
Nec mysteria Gog et Magog sub Leone	2300
Spiritualis belli intelligentia.	2300
Iste qui edoctus intelliget	2300
Et qui in fine intellectum habebit a Deo	2300
Hoc numero inveniet sermones	2300
Sermones istius Latinos	2300
Signatos spiritu sancto	2300
Illeque inveniet ex Numero hoc	2300
Sermones istos in fine dierum.	2300

Our good Lutheran next proceeds to find the Christian Mysteries in his same great number in the following remarkable *cabalistica* :—

2300.

Ihesus, Ihesus est filius Dei	2300
Et filius ejus unigenitus	2300
Ille sapientia, sapientia dei Patris	2300

Ejusdem patris omnipotentia	2300
Ecce ille patri consubstantialis	2300
Ecce enim vere genitus non factus	2300
Ecce est filius genitus ab æterno.	2300
Nunc ipse filius dei homo factus	2300
Est. Et idem incarnatus de virgine	2300
Et ille nunc est filius hominis	2300
Et ipse nunc filius virginis	2300
Atque filius sine viri semine	2300
Semen Abrahæ Davidis Mariæ a spiritu	2300
Et idem semen mulieris a Deo benedictum.	2300
Ecce ipse vir a spiritu sancto	2300
Christus est, ac Deus et Homo	2300
Nunc Ihesus est unctus	2300
Unctus a patre ac a spiritu	2300
Unctus Rex gloriæ a Deo patre	2300
Ecce unctus est Spiritu dei	2300
Spiritu a quo conceptus.	2300
Verbum patris est victima	2300
Victima vera filius virginis	2300
Ecce agnus in cruce offerendo se patri	2300
Fit victima dei, et est pontifex	2300
Est summus sacerdos domini	2300
Summus sacerdos dei patris	2300
Est victima dei et Justificatio.	2300
Agnus verus tulit peccata	2300
Tulit peccata passione morte	2300
Moriens moriendo tulit peccata	2300
Tulit peccata iste redemptor	2300
Deus salutis tulit peccata	2300
Tulit peccata filius dei sacerdos	2300
Hic sacerdos morte tulit peccata.	2300
Filius virginis Mariæ placat iram	2300
Iram dei placat morte sua ac salvat	2300

Agnus occisus est Victor 2300
En Victor mortis diaboli ac inferni 2300
Iste idem Victor peccati et mundi 2300
Moriens fit Victor in morte 2300
Morte ac vita sua justificat. 2300

Nunc ille in gloria dei patris sui 2300
A dextris dei Rex est ac sacerdos 2300
Vere Jhesus est Rex regum 2300
Ecce Rex et Dominus Dominantium 2300
Hic Rex Ihesus unigenitus dei 2300
Protegit nos ac pios salvat 2300
Impios quoque justificat. 2300

Iesus nobis est salvator 2300
Iesus ille natus ex virgine 2300
Est nobis salvator de virgine 2300
De virgine Maria nobis est salus 2300
Salus est, salvat credentes 2300
Agnus est et lux piorum 2300
Iter et Via, Veritas et Vita. 2300

Nunc princeps ille magnus Ecclesiæ dei 2300
Reficit nos proprio corpore 2300
Proprioque sanguine suo 2300
Ac fovet verbis suis solis 2300
Verbis omnipotentiæ Jesus 2300
Facit hoc verus Deus noster 2300
Magnus Dominus omnipotens. 2300

Dominus credentes justificat 2300
Sola fide gratis justificat orbem 2300
Ipse propter semetipsum 2300
Sola fide Evangelii sui justificat 2300
Et ecce justificat filius hominis 2300
Justificat nos Nazarenus 2300
Ac sola fide justificat deus et homo. 2300

Audite impii inclusa mysteria 2300
Audite.   Passio filii dei justificat 2300

Passio Christi. Oblatio in cruce	2300
Et Passio filii dei, filii dei Jesu Christi	2300
Ac sanguis fusus filii hominis	2300
Sanguis filii dei nos justificat	2300
Et illa est fides, Et ea hac fide justificat.	2300
Ecce Jhesus Christus filius dei	2300
Pro nobis natus passus	2300
Idem passus ac idem sepultus	2300
Hic descendit ad inferna, Hic ascendit in cœlum	2300
Hic tertia die a morte resurgens	2300
Idem resurgens ascendit in cœlum	2300
Idem sedet a dextris dei patris. Amen.	2300

Having thus filled up the mysteries of Christ from the great number, he proceeds to show the mysteries of Antichrist from it as well. He acts on this principle with the other numbers of Daniel and John throughout.   He seems to assume that they contain an antithesis of Christ and Antichrist, a popular Lutheran theory.

2300.

Ecce Evangelium a spiritu sancto	2300
In scripturis manifestum	2300
Id sigillatum est in numeris dei	2300
Evangelium a patre et ab æterno filio	2300
Istud persequuntur	2300
Bestia, et ista Meretrix peccati	2300
Ecce hæc fit ebria, ebria sanguine sanctorum dei.	2300
Fidem fidelium deformavit papatus	2300
Papatus fidem istam dei vastat	2300
Fidem justificationis dei patris	2300
Fidem justificationis in regno filii	2300
In regno filii dei in montibus Israel	2300
Fidem istam damnat hæc meretrix Roma	2300
Et fit istud in Ecclesia sancta filii dei.	2300

Ecce hæc est illa abominatio in loco sancto 2300
Ecce Ecclesia ac Antichristi statuta 2300
Et ecce Ecclesia ac regnum impii papatus 2300
Ecce Ecclesia ac Antichristi Romani canones 2300
Et ecce Ecclesia ac iniquus papatus 2300
Ecce Ecclesia ac jura illa mundani papatus 2300
Et ecce Ecclesia ac sedens in ea jam diu homo peccati. 2300

Ecce in Templo filius perditionis 2300
Homo peccati sedens in Templo Ecclesiæ dei 2300
Ecce Rex est Romæ triplici corona 2300
Is Rex est Antichristus 2300
Et ille Antichristus Papa Romæ 2300
Est homo peccati ac adversarius dei 2300
Hic enim regnum Christi vastat. 2300

Et ecce Lutherus doctor gratiæ 2300
Doctor gratiæ in tempore suo 2300
Revelabat Evangelium dei totum 2300
Evangelium fidei, Evangelium Christi 2300
Ecce stabit et docebit verba dei manifeste 2300
Fidem et Evangelium filii hominis docebit 2300
Hoc opere dei factus est doctor a Deo. 2300

Revelatur homo Leo decimus Papa 2300
A revelato isto Antichristo 2300
Destruitur doctrina Romæ 2300
Ecce revelabitur os Leonis, Papa Leo 2300
Damnat nos credentes ac Christum 2300
Pontifex ille Bulla vanitatis 2300
Damnat Leges domini, opera bona, dilectionem. 2300

Evangelium ex patre interficiet 2300
Papatum spiritu Christi 2300
Ex spiritu oris Christi 2300
Destruitur Synagoga Diaboli 2300
Babylon hæc apparentis Papatus 2300
Regnum Papatus et homo peccati 2300
Ac ista Babylon cecidit, nec resurget 2300

Abominatio Romana visa in Templo dei	2300
Est signum Christi, id apparet	2300
Et est signum Danielis certum	2300
Et qui legit signum intelligat	2300
Id Christianis est signum filii dei	2300
Abominatio est papatus et Papa	2300
Ea enim est abominatio desolationis.	2300
Signum filii hominis ac domini dei in cœlo	2300
Manifestum erit patebit in cœlo	2300
Hoc erit in angustia temporis	2300
Et de cœlis revelabitur clamor ille	2300
Sponsus dominus venit	2300
Excite obviam sponso repente	2300
Et vide, Diem et horam finis nemo sciet.	2300
Et ecce extrema persecutio Ecclesiæ	2300
Ac ultima patientia sanctorum	2300
Deinde dies et hora finis. En illa nemo sciet	2300
Ecce mox consurget MICHAEL FILIUS DEI	2300
Ac verbo resurgent mortui	2300
Canente simul tuba novissima	2300
Veni domine Jesu Christe. Ac cito. Amen.	2300

Having thus considered the number 2300 taken from Dan. viii. 14, our cabalist goes to the last three verses of this Book of Daniel, and takes from them the two mystical, prophetic, and comforting numbers 1290 and 1335, and proceeds to examine them cabalistically each in exactly ninety-nine different Latin clauses in the following manner :—

1290.

Patebit liber Danielis	1290
Ac apparebunt in Daniele	1290
Numeri beati Danielis	1290
Ambo numeri dierum	1290
Duo numeri finis	1290
Et veri numeri dei	1290
Ac verba domini signata.	1290

Ecce obsignata sigillata	1290
Signata Numeris	1290
Et his numeris dei	1290
Sunt verba Angeli	1290
Ad finem loquentis	1290
Ecce sunt a Deo clausa	1290
Et signata a beato Daniele.	1290
Tempora amborum	1290
Numerorum de fine	1290
Ambo mysteria de fine	1290
De fine mundi erunt	1290
Et hæc sunt certa	1290
Clausa lingua latina	1290
Latina sunt ac clara.	1290
Ecce signata Babylon magna	1290
Et Meretrix latina	1290
Papatus orbis	1290
Orbis caput dolo	1290
Dolo vastans fidem	1290
Fidem Ecclesiæ dei ineffabiliter	1290
Hæc Babylon in Templo.	1290
Et ecce abominatio in Daniele	1290
Babylone anterior	1290
Ac anni plane priores	1290
Et dies ablati sacrificii	1290
Ante 666 ac Papam	1290
Ecce post Tempora	1290
Apostolica ipsa ac fidei.	1290
Sed ecce ea mala fidei confusio	1290
Fidei fuit ac operum	1290
Ipsa abominatio impia	1290
Et Ecclesiæ contraria	1290
Ipsa confusio magna	1290
A Tempore fidei Jhesu	1290
A fide Christi designata.	1290

Ecce finem habent Tempora 1290
Sumpta ab anno 228 1290
Ac finita fidei confusio 1290
A revelato Papa Leone 1290
Decimo, Papa illo sedente 1290
In Templo dei vivi 1290
Ecce deinde clarissima Ecclesia. 1290

Revelatur Leo fide 1290
Fide, Sexto anno Decimi 1290
Et Leo, ille homo peccati 1290
Leo est, Est Romæ 1290
Et Leo, Leo rugiens 1290
Ecce rugit hic decimus 1290
Bulla vanitatis. 1290

Et ideo apparebit fides 1290
Fides a deo, misericordia dei 1290
Fides hæc sanctissima 1290
Ecce hanc docebit Propheta 1290
Ipse Martinus 1290
Et homo ille Antipapa 1290
Docebit hic Evangelium dei. 1290

Ecce liber clausus a deo 1290
Docet hæc mysteria 1290
Ecce vir ille Jhesus 1290
Sanctitate munda 1290
Conceptus est 1290
Nemo ita sine peccato 1290
Nisi hic filius Mariæ. 1290

Ille nunc est homo 1290
Sed deitate filius dei 1290
Illeque Deus ac homo 1290
Ac homo de spiritu 1290
Inde filius hominis 1290
Et idem ex semine David 1290
Dominus semen Abrahæ. 1290

Ecce semen sanctum a deo	1290
Seipso benedictum	1290
Ex hoc justitia	1290
Et benedictio fidelium dei	1290
Hic filius dei victima	1290
Hinc crucifigitur	1290
Inde filius dei Agnus.	1290
Crucifixus ille	1290
Vere salvator	1290
Et salus æterna	1290
Hinc agnus dei sacerdos	1290
Sacerdos moriens	1290
Ut is redimeret	1290
Nos morte sua.	1290
Sed hic resurgens	1290
In cœlos procedens	1290
Regnat Rex gloriæ	1290
Ac a dextris dei defendit	1290
En hic salvat nos fide	1290
Ac ea sola justificat	1290
Et gratia adjuvat	1290
Nos miseros. Amen.	1290

Next comes the number of which it is said : "Blessed is he that waiteth and cometh to the thousand three hundred and five and thirty days " (Dan. xii. 12).

1335.

Ista summa admiranda	1335
Aperit clara et vera	1335
Et magna testimonia	1335
Evangelii in fine dierum	1335
Dicebat vero Angelus	1335
Daniel claude sermones	1335
Et clare stabis in fine.	1335

Et summa numeri	1335
Revelat literis	1335
Fidem justificantem	1335
Quam aperte negant	1335
Papæ mancipia iterum	1335
Fides sola sine opere	1335
Fides est. Hæc salvat.	1335
Ecce Jesus Magister	1335
Ac doctor verus	1335
Istud hoc ita docet	1335
Hunc audite. Ecce pater	1335
Dixit, hunc audite	1335
Is Jesus Lux	1335
Ac homines tenebræ impiæ	1335
Jesus solus	1335
Salus est Ecclesiæ	1335
Ipse salus certa	1335
Salus pacis grata	1335
Illa salus summa	1335
Ac salus hæc revelata	1335
Salus sola fidelis.	1335
Ecce ex virgine sancta	1335
Incarnatus est	1335
Iste conceptus	1335
Est de Spiritu	1335
Idem natus ex Maria	1335
Homo est, ac filius Dei	1335
Ac vere Deus et homo.	1335
Hic homo justificat	1335
Veritate Evangelii	1335
Et idem Christus	1335
Homo omnipotens	1335
Nos etiam salvat	1335
Idem Jesus victima	1335
Agnus dei ac Deus ipse.	1335

Ille fuit in morte	1335
Et mortem evicit	1335
Fuitque sub Lege	1335
Et idem legem adimplevit	1335
Sic legem nobis vicit	1335
Sensit tamen iram	1335
Et idem iram dei abolevit.	1335
Vicit redemptor	1335
Moriens in morte .	1335
Et iste victor	1335
Vita revixit	1335
Hic ascendens descenderat	1335
Nam ecce in inferno fuit	1335
Ecce ibi vicet infernum. .	1335
Ecce idem ascendit in cœlum	1335
Ac nunc locum parat	1335
Singulis electis	1335
Istis abiens adest	1335
Victor ille mundi	1335
Et suos liberat	1335
A dextris dei orat	1335
Ecce hæc verba fidelissima. Amen.	1335

Next the antithesis :—

The Mysteries of the Antichrist.

In hac computatione	1335
Sunt plurima	1335
Verba sigillata Ecclesiæ	1335
Literæ ejus latinæ	1335
Aperiunt sigilla ac Mysteria	1335
Mysteria agni et Papæ	1335
Christi et Papæ clara.	1335

Et hæc est calculatio	1335
Certa sanctissima	1335
Et vere clarissima	1335
Hæc indicat Christum	1335
De numeris sacris	1335
Eadem Antichristum indicat	1335
Secreta Antithesi.	1335
Papatus Babylon	1335
Est odiosa Babylon	1335
Ac illa est odiosa Roma	1335
Id nomen Sigillatum	1335
Ipsum in fronte	1335
Hic id nomen Papatus	1335
Et nomen Papæ Leonis.	1335
Apparebit primo Leo	1335
Leo Papa signatus	1335
Istud sigillum	1335
Sigillum nominis	1335
Nomen ejus implet	1335
Et perfecte perficit	1335
Leo, Leo Papa, Leo Decimus.	1335
Ecce 666, Et sigilla	1335
Bestiæ. Et decem Cornua	1335
Cornua, Os Leonis	1335
Et illa septem Capita	1335
Ecce Bestia maxima mundi	1335
Ac in ea vires draconis	1335
Et ecce sigillata decem diademata.	1335

Next, the two great numbers of Daniel, 1290 and 1335, are taken
together. Our author remarks that if Daniel's greatest number, 2300, be
taken, and *duo* added to it *per Cab. Trig.*, we get 2625, which is the
sum of the two (*duo*) numbers 1290 and 1335.

1290 + 1335.

2625.

Hi numeri sunt numeri beati Danielis	2625
Ipsi duo numeri visionis Danielis	2625
Sunt verba latina signata et clausa	2625
Et sunt verba numeris sigillata	2625
Et ecce duo numeri sunt sermones	2625
Sermones clausi visionis Danielis	2625
Et ista sermones dei sunt latini.	2625
Hi numeri sunt duo numeri finis	2625
Qui duo numeri revelabuntur	2625
De Christo redemptore, ac Antichristo	2625
Quos præteribunt plurimi	2625
Donec veniat consummatio regni mundi	2625
Et donec numeris fiat revelatio finis	2625
Et ecce in fine dierum intelligent plurimi.	2625
Dictum est ab angelo, In fine dierum stabis	2625
Daniel claude sermones ac verba domini signata	2625
Hos tales sermones claude numeris	2625
Absconde verba, claude librum pluribus	2625
Librum in fine tantum manifestandum	2625
Eum totum absconde sub numeris	2625
Evangelium enim filii dei est in numeris dei.	2625

The doctrine of the Trinity is next elaborately evolved :—

Ecce unitas et Trinitas essentiæ dei	2625
In ista unitate dei, tres personæ dei	2625
Deus pater, Filius dei, ac Spiritus	2625
Tres personæ simplex essentia	2625
Ac persona personæ coæqualis perfecte	2625
Qualibet persona dei plena ac tota deitas	2625
Hæc illa personarum Trinitas Deus.	2625

Pater est æternitas, æterna deitas   2625
Et filius dei cum sancto spiritu   2625
Et eadem deitas unitas et Trinitas dei   2625
Ecce a patre filius essentia æternus   2625
Hic idem filius non factus sed genitus   2625
Ideo ille filius genitus est ab æterno   2625
Genitus veraciter ante omnia sæcula.   2625

Essentia patris omnipotentis   2625
Et filii dei, Et eadem essentia Spiritus   2625
Spiritus sanctus patris   2625
Et spiritus filii dei, ab utroque   2625
Non factus, nec genitus, at procedens   2625
Ipse est procedens ex patre et filio,   2625
Ipse idem vere Spiritus amborum.   2625

Jhesus filius dei, Verbum patris   2625
Hic filius dei Deus, et factus est homo   2625
Filius hominis ex virgine natus   2625
Filius Mariæ, ex Maria virgine natus   2625
Idem filius est ab ea de Spiritu sancto   2625
Conceptus est incarnatus est   2625
Ihesus iste filius dei naturalis.   2625

Hic Jhesus est homo sine viri semine   2625
Ecce conceptus est ex virgine sancta   2625
Solus est conceptus de virgine   2625
Nemo sine peccato nisi Jhesus agnus dei   2625
Jhesus Deus, Jhesus homo factus   2625
Jhesus Christus Abrahæ, Davidis, Mariæ   2625
Semen mulieris Abrahæ a deo promissum.   2625

Jesus passus est pro nobis   2625
Et hic Jesus salus et Salvator   2625
Filius dei tectus deitate, filius hominis   2625
Filius dei passus sepultus   2625
Jesus Nazarenus est filius dei   2625
Et Filius dei ex virgine de spiritu   2625
Hic Jesus passus, descendit, ascendit.   2625

Ille filius flagellatus tulit peccata   2625
Ille homo flagellatus consputus   2625
Hic spinis crudeliter coronatus   2625
Et crucifixus et mortuus   2625
Surrexit tertia die pro nobis   2625
Et surrexit dominus a morte   2625
Hic ascendens sedet a dextris dei patris.   2625

Iste unigenitus filius dei a patre   2625
Lavat nos sanguine, sanguine suo   2625
A peccatis, sine operibus nostris   2625
Ac intercedit pro peccatis nostris.   2625
Ecce factus est justitia nostra   2625
Et justificat nos filius hominis   2625
Filius hominis a dextris patris.   2625

Jesus Christus Rex sacerdos   2625
Et dominus in gloria dei patris sui   2625
Dominus et princeps magnus Ecclesiæ dei   2625
Iste Dominus Deus et Rex Regum   2625
Iste dominus dominantium regnans   2625
Pater futuri sæculi placans iram dei   2625
Jesus dominus Deus salvator.   2625

Vere salvator solus Jesus   2625
Vere salvator ac vere Deus et homo   2625
Victor est et idem Victor regnat   2625
En victor legis, Diaboli, mortis ac inferni   2625
Victor peccati, peccati Victor ac mundi   2625
Ille victima pro peccatis nostris   2625
Et victima sanctus sanctorum   2625
Et occisus est agnus dei verus   2625
Et dominus Jesus crucifixus.   2625

Jhesus Christus est salus   2625
Agnus verus sacerdos unicus   2625
Et salvator de Spiritu sancto   2625
Hic Jesus venit.   Et veniet in gloria dei   2625

In fine sæculorum, cum apparuerit   2625
Cum apparuerit similes ei erimus   2625
Et vita æterna similes ei erimus.   Amen.   2625

Next comes the usual antithesis :—

Antichrist and the Last Days.

Evangelium revelat Antichristum   2625
Et idem Antichristus Papa Leo Decimus   2625
En Papa revelandus, et nomen Papæ Leonis   2625
Fit, Leonis, Adriani, Clementis, Pauli, Julii   2625
Sedebunt illi successive.   Væ, Væ, Væ,   2625
Væ tibi Papa Romæ, Væ tibi Cæsar, Væ Bestiæ   2625
Væ, Væ, Væ, Ceciderunt Capita quinque.   2625

Primo apparebit Leo.   Secundo Adrianus   2625
Deinde Clemens, Paulus, Julius.   Ac alii in fine   2625
Hæc est revelatio filii iniquitatis   2625
Revelatio filii perditionis manifesta   2625
Hominis peccati et Antichristi Leonis   2625
Et clare apparuerunt decem diademata Bestiæ   2625
Id est: Decem Leones Bestiæ, certa calculatione. 2625

Ecce dominus interficit Papatum Romæ   2625
Eum Papatum destruet Jhesus   2625
Destruet Episcopos Papatus   2625
Ecce destruet hunc Antichristum dei   2625
Ac idem destruet eum adventu suo   2625
Peribit Spiritu oris Christi   2625
Et nunc ille sine manu conteretur.   2625

Interficiet hunc Evangelium a Christo   2625
Ecce Evangelium Lutheri confirmatum a Deo   2625
Et ecce confirmatum in Scripturis   2625
Libri Veteris ac Novi Testamenti dei   2625
Est enim fides revelata patris et filii   2625
Fides revelata a spiritu in papatu   2625
Sola fides Lutheri salvat credentes.   2625

Fides justificationis sola salvat   2625
Ille articulus justificationis   2625
Est a spiritu sancto dei patris   2625
Est Evangelium gratiæ dei patris de filio   2625
Est scientia dei de filio suo crucifixo   2625
Hæc fides justificationis justificat   2625
Et fides Christi gratis justificat.   2625

Fides filii hominis justificat ac salvat   2625
Ac ecce hæc sola justificat ac sola salvat   2625
Hæc fides Lutheri justificat credentes   2625
Ac ea sola solus Jesus justificat   2625
Et hæc fides revelat mysterium Papæ   2625
Ac revelat fidelibus abominationes ejus   2625
Abominationes Meretricis Papatus.   2625

Ecce revelatur signata Meretrix   2625
Babylon magna Meretrix in Apocalypsi   2625
Ecclesia Papistica Meretrix Babylon magna   2625
Mysterium in fronte, Babylon magna   2625
Et secretum, in fronte meretricis   2625
Poculum aureum in manu, Papæ decreta   2625
Ecce hic calix aureus in manu meretricis.   2625

Mundabitur Ecclesia domini sub Leone decimo   2625
Sub Leone, anno sexto Papæ Leonis decimi   2625
Mundabitur scientia in spiritu   2625
In spiritu sancto mundabitur   2625
Ecclesia.   Eo anno domini 1518.   2625
Sub Leone.   Ab Angelo volante per medium cœli   2625
A Luthero Antipapa Sophistarum.   2625

Postea erit persecutio ultima   2625
Ultima persecutio sanctorum   2625
Et ultima persecutio verbi domini.   2625
Patientia sacra sanctorum ultima   2625
Tempora post Lutheri Tempora   2625

Sunt ultima tempora nostra 2625
Et illa omnia omnes impii non intelligent. 2625

In ipso fine dicent, Pax et securitas 2625
Illa dicent principes persecutores 2625
Persecutores Ecclesiæ novissimi 2625
Et manifestabitur signum cœleste 2625
Signum filii hominis firmatum in cœlo 2625
Id erit signum adventus Christi 2625
Tunc ipse filius hominis apparebit 2625
Et ecce apparebit canente tuba novissima 2625
En de die illo et hora nemo mortalium sciet. 2625

Revelabitur clamor media nocte factus 2625
Et clamor ille tuba ultima et septima 2625
Tunc exite. Ecce sponsus venit 2625
Venit, Exite obviam venienti domino 2625
Exite, Ite obviam sponso sponsæ 2625
Sponsus venit, Exite, Ecce jam finis 2625
Finis mundi hujus, Veni domine Jesu 2625
Domine Jhesu Christe, et festinanter 2625
Ecce ego venio cito, Veni domine Jhesu, Fit. Amen. 2625

BIBLIOGRAPHY

BIBLIOGRAPHY

1582. ELCHANON PAULUS VON PRAG.

MYSTERIUM novum. | Ein new herzlich | und gründtlich beweisz nach der He|breer Cabala dasz aigentlich der Name und | Tittel desz Herrn IESV CHRISTI Gottes|Son in den fürnembsten Propheceyungen von | Messia, verdeckt in denn Hebraischen | Büchstaben bedeutent ist.| Gestellet durch | Elchanon Paulum von Prag, | welcher zuvor bey den Juden ist ein für|nehmer, hochgelerter Rabi | gewesen, und geheissen Rabi | Elchanon, sich aber in dem Namen Jesu Christi Tauffer|lassen im waren Christlichen Glauber, in | Polen in der Statt Chellim. | Sampt einer ernstlichen Vermanung des Authoris an alle Juden. | Mit Röm. Kay. Mt. etc. Gnad und Privilegien.|

Gedruckt zu Wienn in Österreich, bey | Michael Apffel zum grünen Röszle in der Schuelstrassen.

ANNO MDLXXXII.

Sign. a—c_4 and A—H_4 in 4to = 88 pp.

1621. ANATHEMATA | B. CONRADO.|
Placentino Anchoritæ | dicata.|
Et de Anagrammatis
        Supputationibus }Numericis.
        Oraculis

Synopsis.
Placentiæ | Typis Alex. Bazachii | MDCXXI.

153

1621. JOANNES BAPTISTA SPADIUS.

(1) De | Francisco | Sacrato | S.R.E. Cardinali | Anagrammaton Numericorum | Corona | ex Virgilianis Conserta flosculis | aliisque numericis | lemniscata. |

F. Jo. Baptista Spadius à Florentiola Lector | Theol. ordinis Prædicatorum | faciebat. |

(*Ad finem libri.*) Mediolani apud Jacobum Lantonum anno InsIgnIs, atqVe Verè aVreæ MeDIoCrItatIs.

24 pp. in 4to.

1623.

(2) S.R.E. | Triumphus | ab | Urbano VIII. | P.O.M. | actus | Francisco | Cardinali | Barberino | a | F. Jo. Baptista Spadio a | Florentiolâ Theologo | ord. Præd. | D.D.D.

(*Ad finem libri.*) Placentiæ, Ex Typ. J. Ardizzoni, 1623.

73 pp. in 4to.

1645.

(3) De | Ludovico XIV. | Francorum | Rege. | Anagrammata | J. Baptistæ Spadii | Placentini. | Placentiæ. | Apud Jo. Ant Ardizzonum, 1645.

36 pp. in 12mo.

A copy in the Mazarine Library ; the only one I know.

1654. ALCALA Y HERRERA, ALONSO DE.

Jardim anagrammatico de Divinas Flores Lusitanas, Hespanholas e Latinas contem seiscentos e oitenta & tres Anagrammas em prosa & verso & seis Hymnos Chronologicos dividese em seis opusculos nastres linguas consagrase. Ao supremo conselho da Sancta General Inquisiçaô destes Reynes & Senhorios de Portugal.

Autor Alonso de Alcala y Herrera natural da Inclyta Cidade Lisboa.

Lisboa, 1654, 4.

13 ff. prel. 274 pp. and 2 pp.

1671. Joannes Evangelista à Panormo.

Anagrammata | sacra | suavis animæ desuaviatio, | pii Musarum lusus | admodum Reverendi | P. D. Jo. Evangelistæ à Panormo | Prioris Casinensis, & S. T. Lectoris. | Opusculum | alias Typis demandatum sed auctum modo : | cui anagrammata quædam non sacra | accessere. |

Panormi, Ticini Regii & iterum Mutinæ ex | Typographia A. Cassiani anno 1671. | Superiorum Permissu.

4 ff. prel. 178 pp. + 1 err. in 8vo.

1684. *Viennæ Plausus.*

Viennæ | pro soluto | Germano-Polonicis | armis | Othomanico obsidio | Miscellometrici | Plausus. |

Genuæ MDCLXXXIV.

Typis Antonii Casamaræ.   In Platea Cicala. | Superiorum Permissu.

2 ff. + 103 pp. + 1 bl. p. in folio.

1686. San Juan y Bernedo, Francisco de.

Conceptio | Immaculata | Deiparæ Mariæ | Virginis | celebratur V. acrostichidibus | continentibus tria millia Anagrammata | numeralia deducta ex oratione Angelica, | ex ejus Litania, ex Antiphona Salve | Regina, et ex hymno Ave Maris Stella, | ex Alphabeti literis.   Et aliqua Ana | grammata sunt ad examen redacta, ut le | ctor facilius videat utrum pura sint necne. |

A Francisco de Sancto Joanne & Bernedo, Presbytero | Hispano Cappellano celeberrimæ Cappellæ Paulinæ | ubi colitur S.S. B. Mariæ Virginis Imago a | S. Luca depicta in S.S. Basilica | Liberiana S. Mariæ Majoris Romæ. |

Romæ, MDCLXXXVI, 8.

176 pp. in 8vo.

This book really contains 1801 numerical anagrams, of which 1505 are on the Virgin, and 274 on St. Theresia.

1701.

Another edition, much enlarged, was placed at the end of the author's collected works (Romæ, 1701, fol., 2 vols.). It occupies pp. 597-654 of Vol. II., and contains 3799 numerical anagrams on the Virgin Mary, and 1599 in honour of St. Ildephonsus, being a grand total of 5398 cabalistical anagrams. They are generally short and neat. I have selected the Scriptural ones only. Both editions are very rare.

1687. Albricius, Nicolaus.

Esdræ | Leo de Silva | ad cujus concitationem rugitum et verba | vidit incendi totum corpus aquilæ | Imperii Turcici. | Opusculum consurgit | ex D. Scripturis, paucis exceptis, et Esdræ 4, | continens multa notabilia et curiosa | politicis, militantibus omnibusque utriusque | Ordinis apprimè tam utile tam jucundum. |

Auctore | Nicolao Albricio | Nob. Berg. Phil. et Med. D. Ven. |

Variorum passim cum suis dilucidationibus | Hieroglyphicorum ex probatissimis | Auctoribus | accessere Icones, | aptius in presens quam elapsa tempora collimantium. |

Venetiis MDCLXXXVII. Typis S. Curti.

12 ff. prel. and 333 pp. in 12mo.

This curious book belongs to the same class as the *Vaticinia sive Prophetiæ Abbatis Joachimi*, which had a large circulation in Italy towards the end of the sixteenth century, as the many editions tend to show.

It is, however, much more bulky and learned than were either the Prophecies of Joachim or the numerous Prophetic and Hieroglyphic wheels which were published about the same period in Italy. There is some likeness between these latter and the Zadkiel and Old Moore's Almanacs of the present day, and though originally in Latin, they were made popular by an appended Italian translation and explanation ; and the hieroglyphics, as with Zadkiel and the rest, were a great attraction.

But though there are hieroglyphical figures throughout the work of Albricius, his is a very different style of culture from Old Moore and his followers. He was a patrician, a philosopher, and a man of medical science, which makes it all the more strange that he should write such rubbish as is contained in the 350 pages of his book. Its object is to show that the Emperor Leopold was the Leo de Silva which should utterly destroy the Ottoman power, and he does this by Biblical prophecies, by anagrams, chronograms, an occasional cabala, and similar literary artifices. I have heard English lectures on "things that are shortly to come to pass," illustrated (on the walls) by hieroglyphics from the Apocalypse and Daniel, but they were indeed puny attempts compared to what Albricius gives us in his remarkable book.

1701. SIMON WOLFF BRANDES.

Die geheime Offenbarung des Königl. Propheten welcher in seinem 21 Psalm die Preussische Kröhnung verkündiget, entdecket von Simon Wolff Brandes Schutz-Juden in Berlin.

Berlin, 1701-8.

1710. MAZZA DE CASTANEA, JOSEPH.

F. Josephi | Mazzæ | de Castanea | nuncupati | ex Cappuccinorum | Familia Minoritæ | sacra et arithmetico- | anagrammatica opuscula. |

Neapoli MDCCX | per Joannem Rosellium, typographum hujus fideliss. Civitatis. | Superiorum licentia.

218 pp. + 8 pp. (*ad fin.*).

This remarkable book, unique of its kind, contains three parts, each with an engraved frontispiece :—

1. Fastorum Immaculatæ Puerperæ elogialis heptas.
2. Columbæ Gemitus, Heptas Dolorosa.
3. Fastorum rituale Jubilæum per septem Heptades.

Altogether it contains the enormous quantity of 2093 cabala, of which 371 were metrical, either hexameters or pentameters. My selection was confined to cabala on Bible texts only, and, as it happened, not one of these was a metrical one, so the extreme ingenuity of the cabalistic expositions is not here in evidence. As a *tour de force*, both for quantity and quality, in the cabalistic department of literature, this book holds the record. I know of no copies in England beside my own, neither did I find it in the catalogues of the great libraries of Germany

and Italy.   The book is full of learned allusions, both theological and
classical, and the author tells us he wished to add explanatory notes and
commentaries, but his vow of poverty as a Capucin prevented him.

RIEDERER, JOHANN FRIEDERICH.

Catalogus derer Eintausend funffzig Paragrammatum Cabbalisticorum
Trigonalium welche auf die Gottheit, hiṁlische Cörper, gecrönte Häupter,
Cardinäle, Generalen, Grafen, Stands-Personen, Gelehrte, Kauffleute
Handwercks, und *Privat*—item auf verschiedene sonderbar-beruffene
und sonst *honnête* Leute beederley Geschlechts, &c., &c.   Darbey auch
Städte gantze Nationem, Sectirer, Verräther des Vatterlands, Schwärmer,
Factionem, Mörder, und andere von solchem *Calibre* ohnvergessen sind.
Durch *Égalisirung* Biblischer Texte, oder Strophen aus geistlichen
Gesangen die sich auf ihre Personen, *Conduite* Eigenschafften, Vorhaben,
Profession, Kunst und Gewerbe schicken, ersonnen und nebst einer
ausführlichen Vorrede von der Einrichtung der Paragrammatum, mit
angehängten *apart*-Register nach ohngefehrer Ordnung hiemit nur dem
Nahmen und dem Stande nach *publicirt* werden von Johann Friederich
Riederer.   Norimb.

S. a. et l.   8vo.
Sign. A—H₆ = 124 pp.

Although the title-page has no date and place, the preface
is signed " Nürnberg, 6 Martii Anno 1719."

Printed in the USA
CPSIA information can be obtained
at www.ICGtesting.com
LVHW050732260923
759331LV00041B/440